SKITS AND SHORT FARCES
FOR YOUNG ACTORS

Other books by
Lewy Olfson

DRAMATIZED READINGS OF FAMOUS STORIES
RADIO PLAYS FROM SHAKESPEARE
DRAMATIZED CLASSICS FOR RADIO-STYLE
  READING (Vol. 1 and Vol. 2)
CLASSICS ADAPTED FOR ACTING AND READING

Skits and Short Farces for Young Actors

A collection of humorous one-act royalty-free plays

by

LEWY OLFSON

Publishers   **PLAYS, INC.**   *Boston*

U. S. Library of Congress Cataloging in Publication Data

Olfson, Lewy.
  Skits and short farces for young actors.

  SUMMARY: Nineteen one-act, royalty-free plays suitable for production by schools, clubs, and other amateur groups. Includes production notes.
  1. Amateur theatricals. 2. Children's plays.
  [1. Amateur theatricals. 2. Plays] I. Title.
  PN6120.A50563   812'.5'4   73–10480
  ISBN 0–8238–0150–0

For SUE LAWLESS

Contents

SKITS AND SHORT FARCES
FOR YOUNG ACTORS

My Son, the Prince

A reluctant bridegroom

Characters

KING HAROLD   FAIRY GODFATHER
PRINCE ENGELBERT   PAGE
NANNY, *his old governess*

SETTING: *Throne room of King Harold's palace.*
AT RISE: KING HAROLD *is pacing up and down, watched by* NANNY.

KING (*Abruptly*): What time is it now, Nanny?

NANNY (*Patiently*): It's half-past Wednesday, Your Majesty.

KING: Is that all? It seems later.

NANNY: But Your Majesty, time wouldn't pass so slowly if you'd find something to occupy your mind. Why don't you take a nap? Or read a good book?

KING: Oh, that's easy enough for you to say, Nanny. What difference does it make to you that my son is out making a fool of himself? You can sleep easily enough. But put yourself in *my* position for a minute. The embarrassment of it all! The humiliation! That son of mine is going to make me the laughingstock of the Seven Kingdoms.

NANNY: Boys will be boys, Your Majesty.

KING (*Sinking morosely onto his throne*): Don't I know it! I have three sons. You'd think *one* of them would shape up and amount to something. But, no! Three idiots, that's what I have. Three dunderheads!

NANNY: Now, now, Your Majesty, they're not as bad as that. They're really very good boys.

KING: Ha! King Percival—now *he* has what I call fine, upstanding sons. Regular princes, both of them.

NANNY: I don't think those kids are anything special.

KING: You don't, eh? The oldest—he wanted to get married. So what did he do? Found himself a girl who knew how to turn straw into gold. That boy has brains!

NANNY: But don't forget that he has to put up with that strange little man with the funny name living in his palace.

KING: All right, so he has a little in-law trouble. With a wife who can turn straw into gold, you can learn to live with a little inconvenience. And the younger son, whom does *he* marry? Only the favorite daughter of the richest merchant in all the Seven Kingdoms. And King Percival's younger son is no bargain, you know. Did you ever get a look at that kid's face? A regular beast—but he marries a beauty! *Those* are *sons*! But *my* three—(*He shakes his head in despair.*)

NANNY: Now what's so bad about your boys?

KING: You've got to be kidding. My oldest—my pride and joy—the heir to my kingdom—my Sheldon. Does he hunt? No. Does he fish? No. Does he go in for archery or falconry or jousting, like any normal, red-blooded Crown Prince? No. He reads books! Whoever heard of a prince who reads books?

NANNY: But that's how he mastered the art of black magic,

from studying all those books of his. And if it weren't for his knowledge of magic, Your Majesty, he'd never have found his bride.

KING: Some bride. A girl so lazy, she once slept for a hundred years. A girl with so little ambition, he had to wake her up in order to propose.

NANNY: But she was under a spell!

KING: Spell, indeed! That's just an excuse. She's lazy, I tell you. For a wedding present I gave her one of those fancy household appliances. A spinning wheel. She took one look at it and fainted.

NANNY: Surely, Your Majesty, you have no such complaint to make against your second son's bride?

KING: She's a beautiful girl, true. But who needs those seven dwarfs of hers? Everywhere I go, it seems as if I'm falling over little men. Sometimes I wonder if this place is a royal palace or a Y.M.C.A. And another thing I don't like about her: she's a health food faddist or something.

NANNY: Now, Your Majesty, surely you aren't being fair.

KING: I mean it. The other day I said to her, "Take a piece of fruit, Snow White. Here's a nice apple." Does she say "Thank you," like a civilized person? No. She screams! (*In falsetto*) "It's poison, it's poison!" Believe me, if there were any poison around here, yours truly is the one who'd be swallowing it. (*There is a fanfare offstage.*) Do me a favor, will you, and tell them to cut out that fanfare stuff. I've got a screaming headache as it is.

NANNY: I think Prince Engelbert has come home, Your Majesty.

KING: Well, it's about time.

ENGELBERT (*Entering*): I'm back, Father. (*Waves to* NANNY)

KING (*Sarcastically*): Hail the conquering hero!

ENGELBERT: Oh, don't make fun of me, Father. I've had a tiring day and I'm not in a good mood.

NANNY (*Sympathetically*): That's too bad, dear.

KING: I gather, then, you didn't find the girl you were looking for?

ENGELBERT: Uh-uh. But I'll look again tomorrow. I'll just keep looking and looking and looking . . .

KING: And what if you never succeed? You can't spend the rest of your life just going from house to house like a dictionary salesman. You're a prince!

ENGELBERT (*Glumly*): Sometimes I wish I weren't.

KING: What? You just watch your language in front of me, young man!

ENGELBERT (*Crossly*): Well, I mean it, Father. Commoners don't have to go to all this trouble.

KING: Commoners don't fall in love with glass slippers.

ENGELBERT: I'm not in love with the slipper, I'm in love with the girl who was *in* the slipper.

KING (*To* NANNY): Eight hundred girls at a party, and he has to fall in love with the only party crasher. Eight hundred names and addresses on the invitation list, and he picks the only one with an unlisted telephone number.

ENGELBERT: But she was so beautiful, Father—so delicate, so fragile.

KING: And the others weren't? What about Rapunzel, for instance? Never in my life did I see such a beauty.

ENGELBERT (*Revolted*): All that hair! Yecch!

KING: What about Odette? A neck like a swan!

ENGELBERT: Yeah—and *feathers* like a swan, and webbed *feet* like a swan—

KING: All right. Nobody's perfect.

ENGELBERT: Oh, Father, don't you know what love is? Real,

true, love-at-first-sight love? Weren't you in love with Mother?

KING: With your mother and me it was different. I was a very ugly kid. Everyone called me Toad. Your mother took pity on me and kissed me one night, and suddenly I felt like a prince. But you—you're handsome. You're smart. You're talented. You could have anyone you want. Why do you have to get hooked on a girl who's walking around right now with only one shoe? (*Fanfare from offstage.* KING *turns to* NANNY.) Can't you get them to stop those fanfares, Nanny?

NANNY: I'll go and tell them, Your Majesty. (*Exits*)

KING: Engelbert, listen to your father. Think of all the things I've done for you. You wanted seven-league boots, I got you seven-league boots. You wanted to go away to college, I sent you to Fairyland Institute of Technology. You wanted to join a protest movement, I let you march up and down in front of the palace with a picket sign saying, "Royalty Is Unfair, Monarchy Must Go." It wasn't easy, Engelbert, but I let you do what you wanted. Now I'm asking for one little favor in return: forget about the girl with the size three feet and marry a regular princess. Preferably the kind where they throw in half a kingdom and five hundred green stamps into the bargain.

ENGELBERT: Money, money, money—is that all your generation thinks about? Haven't you any ideals? What about love—art—humanity?

KING (*Pompously*): Fine words harvest no wheat, my boy.

ENGELBERT: What's that supposed to mean?

KING (*Shrugging*): How should I know? I'm trying to be a responsible parent. That's how responsible parents talk.

PAGE (*Entering*): Your Majesty, your Fairy Godfather is here to see you.

KING: Wonderful! Wonderful! You hear that, Engelbert? My Fairy Godfather is here. *He'll* put some sense into that head of yours. (*To* PAGE) Don't just stand there. Show him in, show him in!

PAGE: Yes, Your Majesty. (*Exits*)

KING: Leave it to him, Engelbert. Always there when you need him. That's what I call consideration.

PAGE (*Entering and announcing*): His Fairy Godfather-ship. (PAGE *exits as* FAIRY GODFATHER *enters.*)

GODFATHER: Good evening, Harold.

KING (*Shaking his hand, enthusiastically*): Good evening, Fairy Godfather. Boy, am I ever glad to see you.

GODFATHER: Of course you are. You know I only show up when you're in trouble. Well, Harold, what's the problem this time?

KING (*Pointing to* ENGELBERT): It's him.

GODFATHER: Engelbert? What's wrong with him? He looks O.K. to me.

ENGELBERT (*Pointing to* KING): *I'm* not the problem, *he* is. I want to marry for love—he wants me to marry for money.

GODFATHER: You having financial troubles, Harold?

KING: No, no, nothing like that. It's just that the boy has some crazy idea about marrying a girl with glass slippers whose name he doesn't even know, and I'm trying to talk a little sense into him.

GODFATHER: What's so important about knowing a girl's name?

KING: Look, whose side are you on?

GODFATHER: It's not a question of sides, Harold. It's a question of communication. The boy's in love. Can't you understand that? Don't you remember what it was like to be his age, when you were concerned with love, art, humanity?

KING (*Pacing*): Look, it's not that I'm not sympathetic, but this is a dog-eat-dog world. It's time Engelbert faced up to it and made a solid, responsible marriage.

GODFATHER: Oh, Harold, I expected better than this of you. You were young once yourself.

KING: Young—and foolish. Just because I made mistakes, does he have to make them?

GODFATHER: Mistakes! It sounds to me as if you've forgotten a certain young lady named Goose Girl.

KING (*Gasping*): Ah! (*Mumbling*) No—no . . . I haven't forgotten.

ENGELBERT: Who was Goose Girl, Father?

KING (*Embarrassed*): It's—it's a long story, Engelbert.

GODFATHER: Goose Girl was the most beautiful girl in the whole Seven Kingdoms when your father was a lad, Engelbert. He fell in love with her and wanted to marry her.

ENGELBERT: Then why *didn't* you marry her, Father?

GODFATHER: Because his parents wanted him to make a sensible marriage. They picked out a girl for him—rich, yes, and even attractive—and a Princess of the Blood Royal to boot. "She'll make a man of you," they said to him.

KING (*Hotly*): And she did! She turned me from a toad into a prince! Your mother was a wonderful woman, Engelbert, and don't you forget it.

GODFATHER: But she wasn't the Goose Girl, was she, Harold?

KING (*Brokenly*): No. She wasn't the Goose Girl.

ENGELBERT: What happened to the Goose Girl, Father? Did she die of a broken heart?

KING: No. She married the prince from the next kingdom. Prince Charming. How I envied him. His parents weren't stuffy, like mine! And the Goose Girl and Prince

Charming had seven beautiful children. Oh, they had their ups and downs, I guess; but on the whole, I'd say they lived happily ever after.

GODFATHER: And yet, after all these years, you haven't forgotten.

KING: No, I haven't forgotten.

GODFATHER (*Briskly*): Well, Engelbert, I don't think you'll have any more problems with your father now. Go on with your search for the girl of the glass slipper. I'm sure that someday you'll find her.

ENGELBERT: Do you really think so?

GODFATHER: I'm pretty sure of it. You'll find her, and marry her, and though you'll have your little ups and downs, on the whole you'll probably live happily ever after.

ENGELBERT: Oh, thank you, thank you! I'll resume my search at once! (*He runs out.*)

KING: You're a wonderfully wise fairy godfather, Fairy Godfather. I appreciate your going out of your way for the kid like that.

GODFATHER: Don't give it another thought, Harold.

KING: Do you really think he'll ever find the girl with the glass slipper?

GODFATHER: No doubt of it. But if I were you, just to make sure, I'd track down a girl named Cinderella Watkins, and see that she gets invited to dinner.

KING: Is that the girl? (GODFATHER *nods*.) Cinderella. Nice name. (*Suddenly*) She doesn't live with any dwarfs, does she? And she doesn't take hundred-year-long naps?

GODFATHER: No, this one's a real jewel. She *does* have a thing about mice and pumpkins—but you'll get used to that. Well, I must be off.

KING: But you just got here! Won't you stay for supper?

GODFATHER: You think you're my only godchild? It isn't

easy being a fairy godparent, let me tell you. Now that I've got your problem solved, I have to move on to somebody else.

KING: Oh?

GODFATHER: Yeah. A nut named Midas. He keeps begging me to give him the golden touch—and this time, I think I'm going to do it! (*Quick curtain*)

THE END

Avon Calling!

If Shakespeare were writing today

Characters
JERRY GLOBE, *theatrical impresario*
MARVIN, *his assistant*
WILLIAM SHAKESPEARE, *playwright*
FRANCIS BACON, *would-be playwright*

SETTING: *Office of Jerry Globe, theatrical impresario. Cluttered desk, with typewriter and telephone on it, stands left center. There is a desk chair in front of it, and several occasional chairs right and left. There is a doorway down right.*

AT RISE: JERRY, *hard-boiled Broadway producer type, is seated at his desk. Telephone is ringing.*

JERRY (*Answering phone*): This is the Globe Theatre. Jerry Globe, Manager, speaking. . . . Yes, madam, this afternoon we have a special kiddie matinee: *A Midsummer Night's Dream,* by William Shakespeare. . . . What do you mean, you never heard of him? Why, Will Shakespeare is one of our up-and-coming young playwrights! Also, on the same bill, we have three acts of live bearbaiting. Both features are rated PG, parental guid-

12

ance suggested. . . . Not at all, madam. Thank you for calling the Globe. (*Hangs up.* MARVIN, *a shirt-sleeved assistant producer, enters.*)

MARVIN: Good news, boss. This afternoon's performance is nearly sold out.

JERRY: Terrific, terrific! Of course, I'm not surprised. Every time we put on a play by Shakespeare, we sell out.

MARVIN: Yeah, but we can't go on running the same old plays forever. The public's going to get tired of them. When is Shakespeare going to come up with a new one?

JERRY: I wish I knew! I've been begging him for a new play, but so far—nothing.

MARVIN: Well, these artists can't be rushed, you know.

JERRY: Artist? Shakespeare? Look, that kid's no artist. He's just a commercial hack. That's what makes me so mad. He can grind the stuff out by the mile, if he feels like it. Some of my *other* playwrights—they're artists. Christopher Marlowe, Ben Jonson—

MARVIN: Well, they may be artists, but they're not box office. When we ran Ben Jonson's *The Alchemist,* we couldn't *give* the tickets away. And Marlowe's *Dr. Faustus* didn't even make it to London. It closed in Coventry.

JERRY (*Shaking his head*): I'm afraid *I'm* partly to blame for the *Dr. Faustus* disaster. I thought doctor plays were going to be the big thing.

MARVIN: But Shakespeare is different. *Midsummer Night's Dream*—a sellout. *Julius Caesar*—a sellout. And as for *Macbeth*—we have three road companies doing that.

JERRY: I know, I know. Well, Shakespeare has an appointment with me this afternoon. He should be here any minute.

MARVIN: Is he going to bring in a new script?

JERRY: I don't think so. But I have a couple of ideas of my own to spring on him that I'm sure he won't be able to resist.

MARVIN: I hope he goes for them. We sure can use another smash hit. (*There is a knock at the door.*)

JERRY: Ah, that must be Shakespeare now. Show him in, Marvin, show him in. (MARVIN *opens door to admit* WILLIAM SHAKESPEARE, *a young man, dressed in black and carrying a skull.*)

MARVIN: Come on in, Shakespeare. We were just talking about you.

SHAKESPEARE (*Glumly*): Good morrow, Marvin.

JERRY (*Jumping up, greeting him effusively, all enthusiasm*): Hey, Willie, baby! Great to see you, great to see you! Isn't it great to see Willie again, Marvin?

MARVIN (*Eyeing* SHAKESPEARE *warily*): Yeah. Great.

SHAKESPEARE (*Glumly*): Good morrow, Jerry.

JERRY (*Hurt*): Is that the best you can do?—"Good morrow, Jerry?" Where's the old bounce, the old pizzazz?

SHAKESPEARE (*With an exaggerated sigh*): Ah, to be or not to be . . . that is the question.

MARVIN (*Blankly*): Huh?

JERRY (*Concerned*): What's the matter, Willie? Not feeling well? What's with this "To be or not to be" stuff? Is that any way for England's number one up-and-coming playwright to talk? (*Leads* SHAKESPEARE *to a chair*) Come and sit down, Willie, baby, and tell Jerry what's bothering you. Marvin, go get Willie a cup of coffee.

MARVIN: Sure, Jerry. How do you take your coffee, Shakespeare?

SHAKESPEARE (*Staring at skull; sepulchrally*): Black.

MARVIN (*Doubtfully*): Right. (*He goes out.*)

JERRY: Hey, I'll bet I know what's bothering you: girl

trouble. That Anne Hathaway you've been going with. She's been giving you a rough time, right?

SHAKESPEARE (*Dully*): Wrong.

JERRY: Is it money trouble? You want a little advance on your royalties? Just say the word, Willie, baby.

SHAKESPEARE (*Scornfully*): What care I for money? Who steals my purse steals trash.

JERRY: Then what is it? What, what, what? You're usually so peppy, so alive! But this (*Gesturing*)—this outfit, this skull, this melancholy pose! This isn't you.

SHAKESPEARE (*With a mighty sigh*): Oh, that this too, too solid flesh would melt . . . would thaw . . . resolve itself into a dew. . . .

JERRY (*Shaking his head*): I just don't understand you, Shakespeare.

SHAKESPEARE (*Slamming skull down on desk and jumping up, suddenly animated*): You don't understand me, Jerry? Oh, vassal! Miscreant! Rogue and peasant slave! I'm sick of being a commercial hack writer, *that's* what's bothering me! I'm sick of turning out stuff like *A Midsummer Night's Dream* and *Macbeth* and *Julius Caesar*! I want to write poetry, Jerry! I want to create art!

JERRY (*Horrified*): But *Midsummer Night's Dream* is a sellout!

SHAKESPEARE (*Contemptuously*): It is not worth the dust which the rude wind blows in our face.

JERRY (*Protesting*): *Julius Caesar* made *Variety*'s list of Box Office Top Ten.

SHAKESPEARE (*Scornfully*): Words, words, words! *Julius Caesar* is a tale told by an idiot, full of sound and fury, signifying nothing.

JERRY: *Macbeth*, then! *Macbeth* is going into its third edition in paperback, and we sold the moving portrait rights to Sixteenth-Century Fox. Even Queen Elizabeth thinks it's great stuff. When she saw it, she bubbled over with praise.

SHAKESPEARE (*Bitterly*): A bubble reputation.

JERRY (*Becoming angry*): Now look, Shakespeare, I've put up with about as much of this nonsense as I'm going to. I have you signed to a twenty-play contract, and I'm going to hold you to it.

SHAKESPEARE (*Dramatically*): Methinks I shall go mad! My wits begin to turn! Don't you understand, Jerry? I can't go on grinding out play after play. My brain is drained!

JERRY (*Expansive again*): Is that all that's bothering you? Ideas? Listen, kid, I've got a million of 'em.

SHAKESPEARE (*Doubtfully*): Well . . . let me hear one.

JERRY (*All excitement now*): There's this rich girl, see, named Katharina. And she's a real shrew, see. So even though she's loaded, nobody wants to marry her. Except one guy: Petruchio. He figures he can be twice as mean as Katharina, break her spirit, get her to marry him, and get all her money into the bargain. So he sets out to tame her.

SHAKESPEARE: How does he do that?

JERRY (*Airily*): Oh, I don't know. You can figure that out as you go along. The important thing is to keep it funny, funny, funny. You can call it *No, No, Petruchio,* or *Kiss Me, Katharina*—something breezy.

SHAKESPEARE (*Sarcastically*): Why not just call it *The Taming of the Shrew?*

JERRY (*In disgust*): Because that title just isn't box office, that's why. Well? Do you like my idea?

SHAKESPEARE: I hate it.

JERRY (*Deep breath*): All right, here's another one you might like better. There are these two kids, see. Juliet and Romeo. They fall in love.

SHAKESPEARE (*Sarcastically*): Surprise, surprise.

JERRY: The trouble is, their families hate each other. So Juliet takes this sleeping potion, see . . . and then Romeo finds her asleep, only he thinks she's dead, see . . . so he kills himself . . . and then *she* wakes up and finds *him* dead, so this time she *does* kill herself—

SHAKESPEARE (*Finishing for him*): And we call it *A Comedy of Errors,* and the important thing is to keep it funny, funny, funny. (*Disparagingly*) How do you think up these awful ideas, Jerry?

JERRY: I don't think them up. I get them out of a book. Holinshed's *Chronicles.*

SHAKESPEARE (*Pityingly*): Oh, what a noble mind is here o'erthrown. (MARVIN *enters, with mug.*)

MARVIN: Here's your coffee, Shakespeare. (*Hands mug to* SHAKESPEARE) Boss, there's someone waiting to see you. Says he's a new playwright. Francis Bacon.

JERRY (*In disgust*): Oh, not again! He's been trying to see me for three months.

MARVIN: Shall I send him away?

JERRY: He'll only come back again if you do. No, send him in, Marvin. I'll get rid of him myself. (*As* MARVIN *goes out,* SHAKESPEARE *rises and starts for door.* JERRY *motions him back to his seat.*) Not so fast, Shakespeare. I'm not through with you yet. (SHAKESPEARE *sits down again, as* MARVIN *ushers in* FRANCIS BACON.)

MARVIN (*Announcing, in doorway*): Francis Bacon. (MARVIN *goes out, as* BACON *comes in.*)

BACON: Oh, Mr. Globe, I'm so glad you've agreed to see me at last.

JERRY: Well, don't be *too* glad. I agreed to see you only so I could tell you once and for all that your stuff is hopeless and we can't use it.

BACON (*Crushed, but trying not to let it show*): You—you don't think I have any talent?

JERRY: Look, as a philosopher, I think you're A-number-one. As an essayist, .you're tops. But as a playwright (*Makes thumbs-down gesture*)—zero.

BACON: Yet my fondest dream has been to write plays. Who reads philosophy? Who reads essays? Nobody. The only way to be important as a writer nowadays is to write plays that people will come to see.

JERRY: Don't tell that to me, Mr. Bacon. Tell that to him! (*Indicates* SHAKESPEARE)

BACON: Why? Who is he?

JERRY (*Making introductions*): Francis Bacon—William Shakespeare.

SHAKESPEARE (*Shaking hands*): I'm very pleased to meet you, Frank.

BACON (*Excitedly*): Not *the* William Shakespeare? The author of *Macbeth*? (*Fawning*) Oh, Mr. Shakespeare, I admire you more than just about anybody.

SHAKESPEARE: You do? An artist like you—admires me? A dry jest, sir! My plays are trifles, light as air. But *your* writing—such style! Such wit! Such grace! You're just flattering me when you say you like my work.

BACON: Nay, do not think I flatter. For what advancement may I hope from thee, that no revenue hast but thy good spirits?

SHAKESPEARE (*Enraptured*): Oh, that was beautifully said! (*To* JERRY) Did you hear, Jerry? *That's* the kind of thing I wish *I* could write! (*To* BACON) Do you mind if I make a note of that? (*Writing*) "Nay, do not think I flatter. . . ."

MARVIN (*Rushing in*): Boss! Boss! Emergency down in the theatre!

JERRY: What's up?

MARVIN: Walter Raleigh's backstage, smoking some of that tobacco he's been importing. The stage manager *told* him there's no smoking allowed—but Raleigh's making a terrible scene. He insists on seeing the manager.

JERRY (*In disgust*): That Walter Raleigh! Always losing his head! O.K., tell them I'll be right there. (MARVIN *goes out.*) Look, Bacon, I hate to be unpleasant, but I'm afraid you're wasting your time hanging around here. You'll never make it as a playwright. And as for you, Shakespeare—remember that contract you signed! You sit down at that typewriter and start writing! (*He goes out.*)

BACON: Ah, 'twas ever thus. I want to write plays and they won't let me. You *don't* want to write plays—and they insist. Ah, I fear me I have the green sickness.

SHAKESPEARE (*Repeating the phrase with pleasure*): "The green sickness"! What a perfect phrase for envy!

BACON: Well, it was a real pleasure meeting you, Mr. Shakespeare . . .

SHAKESPEARE (*Shaking hands with him*): Oh, call me Bill, please.

BACON: I guess I'd better go now. Parting is such sweet sorrow that I should say good night till it be morrow.

SHAKESPEARE (*Enchanted*): Oh! "Parting is such sweet sorrow. . . ." (*Suddenly getting an idea*) Say, Frank, you really want to write plays, do you?

BACON (*Eagerly*): More than anything!

SHAKESPEARE: Then how would you like to collaborate with me?

BACON (*Overwhelmed*): You mean it? You—the great Shakespeare—would work with me? That would make us heirs of all eternity! But—but what about Mr. Globe? I'm sure he'd never agree.

SHAKESPEARE: He doesn't have to know a thing about it. We'll just put *my* name on the finished script. But of course I'll divide all the royalties with you.

BACON: Oh, Bill, I'd like nothing better! And I even have an idea for a play that I think might provide the food of sweet and bitter fancy.

SHAKESPEARE (*Overwhelmed*): Ah, wait—let me put that down—"sweet and bitter fancy." (*Writes*)

BACON: The play is about a melancholy prince, in Denmark, whose father has been murdered, and whose mother has married the new king—the very man that did the deed.

SHAKESPEARE (*Enthusiastically*): Ah-h-h! It comes to my ears like a sweet sound. But let's not talk about it—let's get going.

BACON: Yes! If it were done when 'tis done, then 'twere well it were done quickly.

SHAKESPEARE (*Rolling paper into typewriter*): I assume we'll call the play after the prince himself. What's his name?

BACON: I haven't given him a name yet.

SHAKESPEARE: How about Sam? (BACON *frowns, shakes his head*.) Melvin? (BACON *shakes head again*.)

BACON (*Slowly, intensely*): How—about—Hamlet?

SHAKESPEARE (*Trying it out*): Hamlet. Hamlet. (*Decisively*) I like it!

BACON (*With false modesty*): Yes, it does fall trippingly on the tongue, doesn't it!

SHAKESPEARE (*As he types*): Hamlet. Act One, Scene One. (BACON *paces around as he dictates*.)

BACON (*Dictating*): The Scene: Ramparts of the castle at Elsinore. Time: Midnight. At Rise: Francisco at his post. Enter Bernardo. . . . (SHAKESPEARE *is smiling happily, typing quickly. He looks up*.)

SHAKESPEARE: Frank, it's wonderful the way the words just roll out of you, as if you're reciting from memory.

BACON (*Nervously*): The idea of collaborating with you still overwhelms me!

SHAKESPEARE: With you as a collaborator, our fortunes shall move upward and we'll be graced with wreaths of victory! Frank, this above all—to thine own self be true! We will strive with things impossible! The play's the thing! (*Curtain*)

THE END

Meet Miss Stone-Age!

A prehistoric beauty pageant

Characters

ROCKY GRAVEL, *emcee*
GLENDA GRANITE, *last year's winner*
BUNNY BOULDER ⎫
MARCIA MARBLE ⎬ *finalists*
SYLVIA SLATE ⎭

BEFORE RISE: ROCKY GRAVEL *enters in front of curtains to address audience. He is a typical beauty pageant emcee— all toothy smiles and oozing personality. He wears a cave-man outfit of animal skins, plus a black bow tie and a top hat.*

ROCKY: In just a minute, ladies and gentlemen, the judges will have finished tallying their slates, and we'll be introducing the finalists in tonight's Miss Stone-Age Pageant. But first, I want to introduce the girl who won last year's pageant, the girl who, for the past year, has been traveling around as our ambassadress of beauty, intelligence and womanhood. Welcome, please, Miss Stone-Age of 9847 B.C., Glenda Granite! (GLENDA *enters, wearing fur cave-woman costume, dark glasses and very high-heeled shoes, and carrying a huge bouquet of roses. She is not very bright.*) Look! Isn't she lovely, folks? Glenda, it

22

certainly is a pleasure to have you here with us on this, the last night of your reign as Miss Stone-Age.

GLENDA (*Deadpan, reciting earnestly and with difficulty*): As I pass on my crown to you, my beautiful and worthy successor—

ROCKY (*Interrupting*): No, no, Glenda, I'm not the new winner. I'm the emcee. You give that speech later in the program.

GLENDA (*Blankly*): Oh. What do I do now?

ROCKY (*Quickly*): Tell us, Glenda, what were some of the special thrills of being Miss Stone-Age?

GLENDA (*Declaiming*): Some of the special thrills of being Miss Stone-Age were winning the money and the new wardrobe. Especially the money. (*Beaming*) I won lots and lots of money, and that was a very special thrill.

ROCKY: You made some personal appearances, didn't you, Glenda?

GLENDA: Yes. I was present at the official ribbon-cutting ceremony marking the opening of Stonehenge.

ROCKY (*Surprised*): Stonehenge? I don't believe it. You mean they finally got that thing built?

GLENDA: Yup. They did it. Don't ask me how, but they did it.

ROCKY: Well, Glenda, they've just given me the signal that the finalists are lined up backstage, waiting to be introduced, so why don't you say a few final words to the audience.

GLENDA (*Declaiming*): As I pass on my crown to you, my beautiful and worthy successor—

ROCKY: Later, Glenda, later! (*He pushes her off into wings.*) Wasn't she lovely, folks? (*Applauds enthusiastically*) And now, to meet the finalists in tonight's pageant. Will you open the curtains, please! (*Curtains open.*)

*　　*　　*

AT RISE: *The three finalists,* MARCIA MARBLE, SYLVIA SLATE, *and* BUNNY BOULDER, *are seated at center. All three wear fright wigs and shabby fur cave-woman costumes. They should look as unattractive as possible. All three have papier-mâché clubs beside their chairs.*

ROCKY (*Enthusiastically*): Aren't they gorgeous, folks? Let me introduce our three finalists—in alphabetical order, naturally. First, from Upper Siberia, the very lovely Miss Bunny Boulder. (BUNNY *comes forward.*)

BUNNY: I just want to say at this time, Rocky, that I am the happiest girl in the whole world, and I want to thank the judges for picking me as one of the finalists.

ROCKY: That's very sweet, Bunny. (*She returns to chair.*) Next, from Outer Mongolia, the beautiful Miss Marcia Marble.

MARCIA (*Coming forward, waving enthusiastically*): Hi, Mom! Hi, Dad! Hi, Teddy and Lois and Phyllis and Chuck and Larry and Amy . . .

ROCKY: That's enough, dear.

MARCIA: Oh, may I please just say hello to my date for next Saturday night?

ROCKY (*Smiling*): Well, all right.

MARCIA: Hi, Nick and Tom and Ed and Barry and Ralph and Eric and Mark and Allen and Don . . .

ROCKY (*Pushing her into her chair*): That's enough, Marcia. Our final finalist, weighing in at 164 pounds, Sylvia Slate. (SYLVIA, *clasping her hands over her head in boxer fashion, makes a triumphant tour of the stage.*)

SYLVIA: That's me, folks! (*She sits.*)

ROCKY: Now, girls, as you know, there are just two parts left to the competition before the judges decide who will be crowned Miss Stone-Age—the talent exhibition, and the intelligence test. Bunny, are you all set for the talent part of the competition?

BUNNY (*Coming forward*): Yes, I certainly am.

ROCKY: Tell us, what is your talent?

BUNNY: Well, I'm a home ec major, so I have decided to recite for you all an original recipe I created.

ROCKY: Well, I think that's wonderful! Isn't that wonderful, folks? (*Turns to audience and applauds madly*) You go right ahead, Bunny.

BUNNY (*Reciting*): This is a recipe for Brontosaurus Stew. Take eight hundred pounds of freshly killed brontosaurus, and season it with half a dozen lumps of finely grated coal. Preheat your cave to four hundred and fifty degrees, and let the brontosaurus simmer for about three and a half days. Meanwhile, separate sixty-four dinosaur eggs—I like Triceratops eggs best, myself, but you can use Tyrannosaurus eggs if that's what you happen to have. Slice fine a couple of two-year-old elm trees . . .

ROCKY (*Clutching his stomach*): Er, Bunny, I'm afraid our time is up. Why don't you just write the recipe down on a card, and we'll let the judges read it.

BUNNY (*Disappointed*): Oh, all right. (*Sits*)

ROCKY: Now, Marcia, are you ready for your talent exhibition?

MARCIA: Yes, I certainly am, Rocky. (MARCIA *goes to wings, where she gets a huge stone wheel, and carries it down center.*) I would like to present as my talent—this! (*She thrusts the wheel at him.*)

ROCKY (*Staggering under its weight*): What—what is it?

MARCIA (*As though it were obvious*): Why, it's a wheel!

ROCKY: A wheel? What's a wheel?

MARCIA: It's a—it's a sort of a block of stone with the edges sort of rounded off. I invented it myself.

ROCKY: It's—it's very nice, I'm sure, but—well, what does it do? What's it good for?

MARCIA: A wheel isn't *good* for anything. It's just an aesthetic object. I'm a sculptor.

ROCKY: Oh. Oh, I see. (*He doesn't.*)

MARCIA: I invented another sculpture. It's a sort of a pole that I put two wheels on. I call it an axle. It doesn't do anything either. Would you like to see it?

ROCKY: No, no, I'm sure the judges have seen enough. But, just out of curiosity, tell me. What on earth gave you the idea for naming this thing a "wheel"? That's such an odd name for a piece of stone.

MARCIA: Well . . . it looked like a wheel. . . . and it felt like a wheel . . . so what else would I call it? A ball bearing?

ROCKY: Thank you, Marcia Marble. (*Puts down wheel. MARCIA sits.*) And now our final finalist in the talent competition, Sylvia Slate. (*SYLVIA trots to center, waving clasped hands over head again.*) Sylvia, what is your talent?

SYLVIA: I'm going to sing.

ROCKY (*Enthusiastically*): Isn't that wonderful! What are you going to sing?

SYLVIA: It's a song of my own composition. Also, I wrote it myself. (*She sings—off-key—to the tune of "Three Blind Mice," simultaneously doing a very clumsy tap dance.*)
Three blind dinosaurs.
Three blind dinosaurs.
See how they walk.
See how they walk.
They all walked up to the Widow Fink.
She clubbed them to death, so they're now extinct.
You would have done the same thing, I think,
To three blind dinosaurs. (*She bows.*)

ROCKY (*Dumbfounded*): That was terrible. . . . (SYLVIA *picks up her club and waves it at him threateningly.*) Terribly well done! Wasn't it, folks? (*Applauds madly;* SYLVIA *sits.*) I can see the judges are going to have a tough time making up their minds. And now we come to the final stage in the competition—the intelligence test! (GLENDA *enters majestically from the wings, declaiming.*)

GLENDA: As I pass on my crown to you, my beautiful and worthy successor—

ROCKY (*Running to her and turning her back toward wings*): Later, Glenda, later!

GLENDA (*Mimicking him, disgustedly*): "Later, Glenda, later!" (*Exits*)

ROCKY: And now, girls, the intelligence test. I will read the question the judges have selected just once. Then each of you will answer it in turn. (*Turns toward wings*) May I have the envelope, please? (*Hand reaches out from wings holding huge block of stone. Then another hand reaches out with a chisel.* ROCKY *takes items, borrows club from* SYLVIA, *and kneels on floor. He makes an elaborate show of chiseling open the stone "envelope," then stands, holding tiny slip of paper.*) The question you are to answer is (*Reading*): What is a woman's true role in today's society? First, let's hear from Marcia.

MARCIA (*Coming forward, wringing her hands*): Oh, I'm so nervous!

ROCKY: Now, just relax, Marcia, and answer the question. And remember, you only have sixty seconds.

MARCIA (*Panicky*): The question has been asked, what is a woman's true role in today's society? And I am glad that that is the question that has been asked, because there is probably no question that is more important than that question that—er—has been asked. And I would like to answer that question. My answer is (*To* ROCKY)—I'm sorry, could you repeat the question?

ROCKY: Oh, I'm sorry, Marcia, your time is up. But I know the judges were impressed with you anyway.

MARCIA: I'm sure they were, too, Rocky. 'Cause I'm the prettiest. (*Sits*)

ROCKY: Now, Bunny, could we hear your answer?

BUNNY: I think in today's society a woman's place is in the cave. I think that she should devote herself to cooking and cleaning and scrubbing and all the other backbreaking, boring, time-consuming chores that make being a full-time cave-wife such a noble profession. I thank you.

ROCKY (*Applauding enthusiastically*): Wonderful! Wonderful! That's what I call real intelligence!

SYLVIA (*Leaping up*): Oh, yeah? That's what I call real stupidity. And anyone that goes for that line is a male chauvinist Tyrannosaurus rex!

ROCKY (*Taken aback by her aggressiveness*): Well, er, Sylvia, it's your turn. What do you think a woman's role is in today's society?

SYLVIA (*Militantly*): I think all that cave-wife business went out with the ice age. You show me a home where the dinosaurs roam, and I'll show you a very messy house! I think the cave-women of today are the equals of the cave-men, and I think we should stand up for our rights!

BUNNY (*Shocked*): Women equal to men?

MARCIA (*To* BUNNY): Don't listen to her, dear. Next thing you know she'll probably want women to have the vote.

ROCKY (*Indignantly*): I must say I don't think the judges are going to care for what you're saying, Sylvia.

SYLVIA: You know something, Rocky?

ROCKY: What?

SYLVIA: You're gorgeous! (*She conks him on the head with her club. He falls to floor unconscious.*) This one's mine, girls—but there are lots more out there. (*Points to audience*)

BUNNY (*Horrified*): But—we can't go around clubbing any man we happen to like! It's—it's unladylike!

SYLVIA: It may be unladylike, but it sure beats sitting around the cave night after night, waiting for the phone to ring.

MARCIA (*Thinking*): Bunny . . . maybe Sylvia has a point. Why should we let the men do all the chasing? Why don't we do a little selective dating ourselves?

BUNNY: You mean—?

MARCIA: I think Sylvia's right. We've got clubs. Let's use 'em!

SYLVIA (*Egging them on enthusiastically*): Right on, sisters! Go get 'em! (BUNNY *and* MARCIA *shoulder their clubs and go running down steps into audience, whooping.*)

BUNNY: I want one with blue eyes!

MARCIA: He'll never know what hit him! (*They run up and down aisles, pretending to conk men on heads with their clubs.* SYLVIA *watches from stage and cheers them on.* GLENDA *enters.*)

GLENDA (*Declaiming*): As I pass on my crown to you, my beautiful and worthy successor. . . . (*Quick curtain*)

THE END

Great Caesar's Ghost!

Friends, Romans, countrymen . . .

Characters

JULIUS CAESAR   SOOTHSAYER
LUCIUS, *his secretary*   MARC ANTONY

SETTING: *Julius Caesar's office. A desk with a telephone on it stands center. There is a secretary's chair beside it and an executive chair behind it. Several other chairs stand around the room.*

AT RISE: JULIUS CAESAR *is standing near his desk.* LUCIUS *is seated beside desk, holding a stenographer's pad and pencil.*

CAESAR: Lucius, take a letter. (*Dictating*) To Augustus Clodius, President and Publisher, Papyrus Press, Main Street, Rome. Dear Augie: Thank you for your scroll dated the seventh of March. I am delighted to learn that my book, *The Gallic Wars,* has hit the best-seller list. I look forward to receiving your check covering my royalties soon, as I am short of ready cash. Do you have any idea when you will be rendering unto Caesar? Paragraph. As for your suggestion that I consider writing a new book, I cannot make up my mind. Do you really think anyone is interested in my memories of Cleopatra? Personally, I regard that as ancient history. However, if you think there might be a movie sale, I'd be willing to think it over. Sincerely yours, Julius Caesar, Dictator of the Roman Empire, General Triumphant, Best-selling Author, *et cetera, et cetera.* Got that?

LUCIUS: Yes, Caesar. You're a great dictator.

CAESAR: Thank you, my boy, thank you. Now then, what's next on the agenda?

LUCIUS: Your soothsayer is here to see you.

CAESAR: By Jupiter! Is it the fifteenth of the month already?

LUCIUS: That's right—March 15, 44 B.C.

CAESAR: How time flies! Very well, Lucius. Show the Soothsayer in. (LUCIUS *rises, goes to door, opens it.*)

LUCIUS (*Calling out door*): You can come in, Soothsayer. The great Caesar will see you now. (SOOTHSAYER, *a shabby-looking man, enters, carrying a crystal ball.*)

SOOTHSAYER (*Approaching* CAESAR *and saluting in Roman style*): Hail, Caesar!

CAESAR (*With a casual salute*): Welcome, Soothsayer. Glad to see you. Sorry to have kept you waiting, but I had some urgent correspondence to take care of.

SOOTHSAYER: Don't apologize, Caesar. I know what life is like for you dictators—busy, busy, busy.

CAESAR: Yeah, it's a regular Roman circus around here. Maybe from now on you could schedule your appointments for the weekend when I have more time. You could come out to the villa some Saturday.

SOOTHSAYER (*Indignantly*): Please! Irving the Soothsayer does not make house calls.

CAESAR: All right, you don't have to get so huffy. It was just a suggestion. Now, what does your crystal ball have to say to me this month?

SOOTHSAYER (*Striking dramatic pose*): Silence! Silence! I

am about to say the sooth! (*Looks into crystal ball*) Hm-m-m. . . . Very interesting! Caesar, would you like to become rich? The crystal ball shows how you can make a fortune.

CAESAR (*Eagerly*): How? How?

SOOTHSAYER: They're holding races at the Colosseum. Go and bet on Ben Hur in the fifth. He's a sure thing.

CAESAR (*Disappointed*): Oh, I can't. My wife and I have to go to a wedding tonight.

SOOTHSAYER (*Horrified*): A wedding? (*Melodramatically*) No, no! That must not be, great Caesar!

CAESAR: Why not?

SOOTHSAYER (*Intoning*): The crystal ball says, "Caesar, beware! Beware the brides of March!"

CAESAR: But that's silly! What possible harm could befall me just from going to a wedding?

SOOTHSAYER (*Shrugging*): Maybe you'll get hit on the head with the bride's bouquet. All I know is, the crystal ball is seldom wrong.

CAESAR: That's true. Your crystal ball called the last election right, and everyone else got it wrong—even the Gallup Poll. O.K., I'll cancel out of the wedding. Lucius, get my wife on the phone for me.

LUCIUS: Yes, Caesar. (*Goes to phone and dials*)

CAESAR (*Musing out loud*): Maybe I'll go swimming instead. There's nothing like a dip in the Tiber.

SOOTHSAYER: Swimming? Bad idea, Caesar. The crystal ball says, "Caesar, beware! Beware the tides of March!"

CAESAR (*Sourly*): Soothsayer, that crystal ball of yours is just full of warnings today, isn't it?

LUCIUS (*Into phone*): Hello, Mrs. Caesar? Just a minute, please. Mr. Caesar wants a word with you.

CAESAR (*Taking phone from* LUCIUS): Hello, dear, how are you? Listen, I'm afraid I won't be able to go to that wedding tonight. I've got to work late at the office. . . . Yes, dear, I know you bought a new maxi-toga just for tonight. . . . Yes, dear, I know you've been cooped up in the atrium all day and were looking forward to going out, but I just can't make it, and that's that. Oh, one other thing. I wonder if you'd invite Cassius over for dinner one of these days. . . . Nothing fancy—just a Caesar salad. I bumped into him, and he had a lean and hungry look. . . . O.K., dear, I'll see you later. 'Bye. (*He hangs up.*)

SOOTHSAYER (*Admiringly*): Gee, Caesar, you certainly got out of that without a fuss. You should hear *my* wife when I try something like that.

CAESAR (*Grandly*): It's all in knowing how. I just picked up the phone, told her what was what, and that was that.

LUCIUS (*Admiringly*): That's Caesar for you. He called, he convinced, he conquered.

CAESAR (*Pleased*): Say, that's catchy, Lucius! Maybe I'll use it in my next book. Well, Irving? What else does your crystal ball have to tell me?

SOOTHSAYER (*Peering into crystal ball*): Hm-m-m. There's *something* there, but I can't quite make it out. It looks like, "Beware the hides of March." You weren't thinking of investing in leather, were you?

CAESAR (*Impatiently*): Of course not! Can't you get it any clearer than that? (SOOTHSAYER *shakes crystal ball, then sets it down and looks at it closely.*)

SOOTHSAYER: Ah, there it is! "Beware the *guides* of March." You were planning a trip, no doubt?

CAESAR (*Doubtfully*): Well, I was thinking of taking the wife and kids on a tour of Radio City Music Hall—but I can't believe the crystal ball would worry about *that*.

SOOTHSAYER (*Squinting*): Or is it, "Beware the *rides* of March"?

LUCIUS: Maybe it has something to do with your new V-8 chariot with the bucket seats.

CAESAR (*Angrily*): Come on, Irving, for what I pay you, I expect you to come up with something better than this nonsense.

SOOTHSAYER: You have to be patient, Caesar. Rome wasn't built in a day, you know.

CAESAR: That's because I wasn't the construction engineer on the job! (*There is a knock at the door.*) See who that is, Lucius. (LUCIUS *walks to door.*) And as for you, Irving, I want you to come up with a message that makes some sense.

SOOTHSAYER (*Shaking the crystal ball*): It's trying to tell me something—but what? What? That's the LXIV-dollar question! (LUCIUS *opens door and* MARC ANTONY *strides in.*)

ANTONY (*Saluting and declaiming*): Hail, Caesar! Friends, Romans, countrymen, lend me your ears. . . .

CAESAR (*Irritated*): What's the matter with you, Marc Antony? Can't you ever just walk into a room and say hello in plain, ordinary Latin?

ANTONY: Well, gee, Caesar, I like to make a good impression.

CAESAR: Asking people to lend you their ears does *not* make a good impression. It sounds—well, unhygienic.

ANTONY (*Sulking*): You just don't like it when anyone else gets some attention instead of you.

CAESAR: Are you suggesting that I'm not telling you the truth?

ANTONY (*Placatingly*): No, no. Everyone knows that Caesar is an honorable man. But I didn't come here to praise Caesar.

SOOTHSAYER (*Blurting out*): You came to bury him.

CAESAR, ANTONY, *and* LUCIUS (*Outraged*): *What?*

SOOTHSAYER (*Confused; amazed at himself*): Did I say something wrong? I am a soothsayer. I'm not responsible for the sooth I say.

CAESAR: But you *are* responsible for what issues from that crystal ball of yours. Have you figured out yet what it's trying to tell you?

SOOTHSAYER (*Staring into crystal ball, then exclaiming happily*): I have it! I have it!

CAESAR: Well?

SOOTHSAYER: It says, "Caesar, beware! Beware the *prides* of March!"

CAESAR (*Happily*): That's better! Now that's a message that makes some sense!

LUCIUS (*Blankly*): It does?

CAESAR: Of course. It's telling me that just because I'm the dictator, just because I'm the greatest man in all of ancient Rome, I shouldn't be filled with pride and hold myself aloof. I should join my fellowmen in a show of good nature and humility.

LUCIUS (*To* SOOTHSAYER): Is that what the message means?

SOOTHSAYER (*Shrugging*): Look, how do I know? I just tell you what the crystal ball says. If it's interpretations you want, you'd better write to Dear Abby.

CAESAR (*Thoughtfully*): "Beware the prides of March!" You know, Marc Antony, I *have* been a little standoffish with the other guys lately.

ANTONY: As a matter of fact, Caesar, Brutus was complaining of that only the other day. He and some of the other fellows are having a stag party tonight, but they decided not to invite you. They felt you were too high and mighty to join them.

CAESAR: A stag party? What's the occasion?

ANTONY: Oh, no occasion. They're just looking for some excuse to cut up a bit.

CAESAR: Well, I'll show them whether I'm high and mighty or not. Where are they meeting?

ANTONY: They're getting together on the steps of the Senate. Just a little informal gathering, you know. They'll probably go out for pizza later.

CAESAR: Since my evening is free, I say let's join them! (*Chuckling*) "Beware the prides of March!" Good advice, Irving! I don't know what I'd do without you. Coming, Marc Antony? (CAESAR *goes out.*)

ANTONY (*At door, looking out*): Say! There go some of the fellows now! (*Calls out dramatically*) Friends, Romans, countrymen, lend me your ears! (*He goes out.*)

LUCIUS: Whew, *that* was a narrow escape!

SOOTHSAYER (*Heaving sigh of relief*): You can say that again! For a minute there, I thought Caesar was really going to let me have it for not coming up with a message he could understand.

LUCIUS: Yeah, it's a good thing for you you finally got it right. Caesar puts a lot of stock in that soothsaying stuff, you know. Why, if you hadn't given him the right message today, I think it would have killed him! (*Quick curtain*)

THE END

Cinderella Revisited

Recycled glass slippers

Characters

CINDERELLA STEPP
MOTHER
PATTY ⎫
TINA ⎭ *Stepp sisters*
FAIRY GODMOTHER

SETTING: *The living room of the Stepp house, a typical middle-class medieval dwelling. Up center, an archway leads to front door off left and to rest of house off right. Down left is a fireplace with an oversized opening. Above it, on the wall, hangs a mirror. A telephone is on a table.*

AT RISE: CINDERELLA, *dressed in a heavily-patched dress and apron, is pushing a carpet sweeper around room at a frantic pace. Whenever she passes a piece of furniture, she stops sweeping, pulls dustcloth from pocket and begins dusting furiously. After a few moments, sound of a door closing is heard.*

MOTHER (*From offstage*): Girls! I'm home! Patty? Tina? Cinderella? (MOTHER *enters. She is a warm, intelligent matron.*) Hello, Cinderella, darling. What kind of a day did my baby have?

CINDERELLA (*Exasperated*): Mother, please! *Must* you track dirt all over the house? I've just finished vacuuming.

MOTHER: I haven't tracked dirt anywhere. I wiped my feet very carefully on each of the three welcome mats you've spread out in the hall. Besides, I thought you vacuumed the rugs yesterday.

CINDERELLA: I did—but I decided I'd better do them again. You can't be too careful where dirt is concerned. (*She resumes dusting.*)

MOTHER: Stop all that dusting for a minute. I have the most marvelous news. (*Looking about*) Where are your sisters? (*Calling off*) Patty? Tina?

CINDERELLA: Oh, they're probably up in their room. (*Scornfully*) Gossiping about boys and clothes and things. (*She sits down. From her apron she takes potato and paring knife. As she talks, she begins paring, catching peels neatly in her lap.*) Honestly, the things those two can find to talk about!

MOTHER (*A bit worried*): Cinderella, it's *normal* for girls to talk about boys and clothes. I wish *you'd* show a little more interest in . . . (*Her voice trails off as she notices what* CINDERELLA *is doing.*) What *are* you doing?

CINDERELLA: You asked me to stop vacuuming so I could hear your news. You can't expect me to sit here and do nothing, can you?

MOTHER: Do you always carry a paring knife about with you?

CINDERELLA: Usually. Or I carry a jar of silver polish and a few teaspoons. I like to have something to work at while I'm not working.

MOTHER (*Shaking her head*): Sometimes I wish I'd never let you major in home economics, Cinderella. Sometimes I wish you'd just taken up something simple and sensible —like ice hockey.

CINDERELLA (*Outraged*): But Mother! Home economics is my whole life! How can you even joke about such a thing?

MOTHER: I know, dear, I know—but I do wish you wouldn't *drive* yourself so. You act more as though you're a servant than one of my own flesh and blood. (PATTY *and* TINA, *lively, normal teen-agers, enter.*)

PATTY: Hello, Mums. Have a good day?

MOTHER (*Kissing each lightly*): Hello, darlings. My, don't you both look nice.

CINDERELLA (*Huffily*): Humph! You didn't tell me that *I* look nice!

MOTHER (*Taken aback*): I know I didn't, Cinderella. But —er—your dress . . .

CINDERELLA (*Hotly*): There's nothing the matter with my dress! Just because it has a few patches is no reason to look down on it. For one thing, it shows that I know the value of a dollar. Just because something is old and worn is no reason to throw it out.

PATTY (*Sighing*): Oh, there she goes again, talking like a home economics textbook.

CINDERELLA: And for another thing, I'll have you know that each patch on this dress was put on in a different way, so I could practice my sewing. This one is put on with running stitches . . . and this one is basted . . . and this one is all done with French knots. . . .

TINA (*Patting her arm gently*): And they're beautiful, Cinderella. Nobody could ever say you don't know your way around an embroidery hoop.

CINDERELLA (*Scornfully*): I'd like to see either one of *you* get an A in Patch-Sewing with those ridiculous iron-on things you use.

PATTY (*Dryly*): I'd like to see either one of us sign up for a course in Patch-Sewing in the first place!

TINA: What was it you called us down for, Mums?

MOTHER (*Excitedly*): Oh, girls, just wait till you hear! The Prince is giving a ball tonight, and all three of you are invited! Isn't that marvelous? (PATTY, TINA *and* CINDERELLA *look glumly at each other.*) I can see by your expressions that you don't think it's marvelous. Maybe you didn't hear me correctly. The Prince—you know— His Royal Highness? He of the great wealth, the vast real estate holdings, and the bachelor status? He's having a ball tonight for all the unattached maidens of the kingdom. That means you. (*Girls remain unimpressed.*) You're all looking at me in the strangest way. Is my head on backward or something?

PATTY (*Awkwardly*): Mumsy, darling, I'm sure it's going to be a perfectly wonderful party. The trouble is, I already have a date for tonight. Peter the Swineherd is taking me to a concert to hear that sensational new rock group, The Three Little Male Chauvinist Pigs.

MOTHER: I see. The social opportunity of a lifetime comes along, and you'd rather go out with Peter the Swineherd. Well, that just makes your sisters' chances with the Prince all the better. Right, Tina?

TINA: Well . . .

MOTHER: Well what, dear?

TINA: I promised Jack, the miller's son, I'd come over and help him with his homework. He's having a terrible time with Introduction to European Barley.

MOTHER (*Smiling bravely*): Well, I guess that lets you out. Fortunately, I know I can count on Cinderella.

CINDERELLA (*Quickly*): No! No, I can't go!

MOTHER: Surely you don't mean to tell me that *you* have a date for this evening?

CINDERELLA (*Stalling*): No, it's just that (*Brightly*)—if Patty and Tina both have dates, they'll need me to iron their gowns, fix their hair, polish their pearls . . .

PATTY: Don't be silly, Cinderella. You don't have to iron my gown.

CINDERELLA (*Amazed*): You're not going to iron it *yourself*, are you?

PATTY: It doesn't need to be ironed. It's drip-dry and permanent-press.

TINA: And I certainly don't need any help with my hair. I borrowed a wig from Rapunzel, just for tonight.

PATTY: Mums, Cinderella has *nothing* to do tonight, and she'd *love* to go to the ball. Wouldn't you, Cinderella?

TINA: Hurrah for Cinderella! The honor of the family shall be saved!

CINDERELLA (*In a panic*): Me? Go to a ball? Dance? With boys? No, Mother! Please! Anything but that!

MOTHER: But Cinderella, darling, someone from the family just *must* go. One doesn't turn down a royal invitation without risking very serious consequences.

PATTY: That's what R.S.V.P. stands for on royal invitations. Turn the invitation down and "Repercussions Start Very Promptly."

TINA: So it's all settled. Patty and I will go out on our dates, and Cinderella will go to the ball.

CINDERELLA: I just remembered something! Something crucial! Something urgent! Something that can't possibly be postponed another day!

MOTHER (*Suspiciously*): Oh? What's that?

CINDERELLA (*Desperately*): The roof needs fixing! (*She runs out.*)

MOTHER (*Exasperated*): Girls, what *am* I going to do with that sister of yours? Oh, I worry about her so! When is she going to realize that there's more to life than cooking, scrubbing, sewing, and chopping wood? When is she going to give up all this housekeeping nonsense and settle down?

TINA: Give her a chance, Mums. One of these days she'll meet the right fellow, and bam! You'll see a whole new Cinderella.

PATTY: Tina's right. When Cinderella meets the man of her dreams, she'll shape up.

MOTHER: *If* she meets the man of her dreams. But how is that ever going to happen when she won't even go to the Medieval Mixers down at the Y? (*Sighs*) Girls, it's at times like this that I wish—oh, never mind.

PATTY: No, tell us, Mums.

TINA: What were you about to wish?

MOTHER (*Shamefacedly*): Well, you'll think I'm silly. I know none of you young people today go along with the old-fashioned notions, but—well, I was going to wish that Cinderella's Fairy Godmother would lend us a hand.

PATTY (*With a hoot*): Fairy Godmother! Oh, Mums, you've got to be kidding!

TINA: Nobody believes in *them* anymore! Fairy Godmothers went out with Rumpelstiltskin! (FAIRY GODMOTHER *enters through fireplace opening. In addition to her traditional finery and wings she wears black rubber overshoes, the buckles flapping. Her tiara is a bit askew; so is her personality. She is quite blasé.*)

MOTHER (*Delighted*): Fairy Godmother! You came!

FAIRY GODMOTHER: I'd have been here sooner, only I got caught in a traffic tie-up.

MOTHER: Why didn't you just wave your magic wand, make a wish and straighten it out?

GODMOTHER: What? Me? Waste my magic wishes on a bunch of lousy drivers? Do you have any idea what magic wishes *cost* these days? Let me tell you, the overhead is almost enough to make me take up another line of work.

TINA (*Curtsying*): Good afternoon, Fairy Godmother.

PATTY (*Curtsying*): Would you like us to fix you a cup of tea?

GODMOTHER: You can skip the politeness business, if you don't mind. Don't get me wrong. You girls are terrific. I wish Cinderella had half of what you have. But I came here on business, and I'd just as soon get on with it. Would one of you just take my wings?

PATTY (*Helping her off with them*): Here, let me take them. I'll hang them up in the closet.

GODMOTHER: Oh, don't bother. You can just drape them over the back of a chair. (PATTY *does so.*)

MOTHER: Girls, you may go to your room. Fairy Godmother and I have some things we'd like to discuss in private.

PATTY: Nice to see you, Fairy Godmother. And good luck with Cinderella!

TINA: If you can get her to go to the ball, I might even end up believing in you! (*Girls go out.*)

GODMOTHER: That's a couple of nice girls you have there.

MOTHER: Oh, thank you. But it's about Cinderella that I really want to talk to you, Fairy Godmother. You remember that home economics business we talked about a few years ago? Well, I'm afraid it's worse than ever now. Morning, noon, and night, that's all she wants to do. Cook, sew, scrub, clean. . . .

GODMOTHER: I figured it was still going on the minute I came through that fireplace. You've got the cleanest fireplace in Fairy-Tale Land.

MOTHER (*With a sigh*): That's Cinderella for you! She makes us wash the coal before we burn it. It was bad enough when she was an undergraduate majoring in home ec. But then she went on and got her M.S.—Master Seamstress. And *now* she's working on her Ph.D.—Perfect Housewife and Domestic!

GODMOTHER (*Seriously*): I see. She's in worse shape than I thought.

MOTHER: If you could just get her to agree to go to the palace tonight! They're having a ball there.

GODMOTHER: You want her to work in the kitchen, or to wait on table?

MOTHER: No, no! I want her to go as one of the guests! She's been invited.

GODMOTHER (*Surprised*): That's all you want? To get her to accept an invitation to a dance? (*Snaps her fingers*) It'll be a breeze.

MOTHER (*A bit shamefacedly*): Well, there *are* one or two other things . . .

GODMOTHER (*Dryly*): I figured it was too easy to be true.

MOTHER: If you could get her to put on a decent dress—and persuade her to call a taxi. If I know Cinderella, she'll want to go in the hay wagon. And her hair!

GODMOTHER: O.K., O.K., you've said enough. I get the picture.

MOTHER (*Hopefully*): Do you think you can do it?

GODMOTHER: I'll do my best. Why don't you send her in here?

MOTHER (*Gratefully*): Oh, Fairy Godmother, we'll never ask another favor of you. Never!

GODMOTHER: Well, there's *one* other favor you'd *better* ask.

MOTHER: What's that?

GODMOTHER: You'd better ask me to the christening of her first-born child. You neglect to invite a Fairy Godmother to a christening, there's no telling *what* might happen! (MOTHER *goes out.* GODMOTHER *looks at herself in the mirror.*) Well, kid, you sure got yourself some assignment this time! And you thought spinning straw into gold was a tough one! (CINDERELLA *enters reluctantly*.)

CINDERELLA: Mother said you wanted to see me, Fairy Godmother. I can only stay a minute. I just put a dozen pumpkin pies into the oven. Besides, if you're here for what I think you're here for, you're just wasting your time.

GODMOTHER: You think I'm here to try to get you to go out once in a while and meet some young people. Right? (CINDERELLA *nods*.) Wrong!

CINDERELLA (*Taken aback*): Oh!

GODMOTHER (*Sitting down, studying her nails*): I don't care about your social life. It's your professional life I'm interested in.

CINDERELLA (*Puzzled*): My professional life?

GODMOTHER: I understand you're a whiz in home economics. I happen to know of a first-rate job opening in the field, and I wondered whether you'd be good enough.

CINDERELLA (*Excited*): You mean it? You'd recommend me for a real job as a home economist?

GODMOTHER: Well, it depends on your skills. How's your sewing?

CINDERELLA (*Proudly*): Look at this dress! It has thirty-six patches on it—each one put on with a different stitch.

GODMOTHER (*Unimpressed*): Big deal. So you're good on patches. But could you meet a real sewing challenge? Would you be able to—er—whip up a ball gown, say, out of the dining room curtains on fifteen minutes' notice?

CINDERELLA (*Eagerly*): Try me!

GODMOTHER (*Quickly*): Of course, you'd have to wear the dress to a ball after you made it. To be sure it stood up to all the dancing activity.

CINDERELLA (*A bit disappointed*): Oh . . .

GODMOTHER (*Quickly changing subject*): How resourceful are you? Do you waste anything, or do you use every last scrap of raw materials at your disposal?

CINDERELLA (*Uncertainly*): Well, I'm sure I do the best I can.

GODMOTHER: You said you had some pumpkin pies in the oven. What did you do with the pumpkin shells?

CINDERELLA (*Taken aback*): Why, nothing. I—uh—

GODMOTHER (*Quickly*): Could you turn them into a golden coach, using nothing but rubber bands, thumb tacks, and a couple of balls of twine?

CINDERELLA (*Confidently*): I didn't get A-plus in Carpentry Around the House for nothing! I can do it if anyone can!

GODMOTHER (*Firing question at her*): How much time would it take you to make six little footman's costumes, small enough to fit some wild mice?

CINDERELLA (*Proudly*): Twenty minutes, tops.

GODMOTHER: How would you go about recycling household trash into a pair of dancing slippers?

CINDERELLA (*After a short pause*): I'd cut up a couple of empty cola bottles.

GODMOTHER (*Taken aback*): Glass slippers?

CINDERELLA (*Gaily*): Why not?

GODMOTHER (*After a moment*): Cinderella, I think you may be the girl for the job!

CINDERELLA (*Avidly*): Oh, do you really think so?

GODMOTHER: Tell you what I'll do. I'll make up a little test—sort of a home economics examination. I'll put in all sorts of hard questions—like, what would you do if you suddenly found yourself having supper with a prince, and you didn't know which fork to use? And, what would you do if you had to be home from a party by midnight, but the host wouldn't let you go? Stuff like that. Then we'll see if we can find a real-life situation for you to test yourself in. If you pass the test, the job is yours! Is it a deal?

CINDERELLA (*Confidently*): I can pass the toughest home economics test you can invent, Fairy Godmother. It's a deal!

GODMOTHER: But remember. You have to do just what I tell you—even if it's a bit difficult at first.

CINDERELLA: If the job is good enough, I won't hesitate. It *is* a good job, isn't it?

GODMOTHER: Oh, yeah, the job is terrific. Seven dwarfs I know, living in a cottage in the woods—they're looking for a housekeeper.

CINDERELLA (*Ecstatically*): It sounds perfect! What do I do first?

GODMOTHER (*Dryly*): First, get those pies of yours out of the oven. I smell burning pumpkin.

CINDERELLA: Oh, my pies! (*She runs out.*)

GODMOTHER (*Picking up telephone*): Get me Poison Apple 6-7044. . . . Hello, may I speak with Snow White, please? This is her Fairy Godmother calling. . . . Hello, is that you, Snow? . . . Listen. About that job over at the Seven Dwarfs'—I think you'd better grab it. . . . Yes, I *did* talk to someone else about it, but I think she has other plans. She's going out to a party, and unless I miss my guess, by the time midnight rolls around, she won't want anything to *do* with housework. She's going to be too busy thinking about getting married! (*Quick curtain*)

THE END

A Couple of Right Smart Fellers

Outsmarting the city slickers

Characters

ZEKE $\Big\}$ *Yankee farmers*
ZACK

HARRIS $\Big\}$ *city slickers*
CARTER

SETTING: *Yard in front of a Connecticut farmhouse. At left center there are two rocking chairs and a small straight chair with a cat sleeping on it. Exit at left leads to farmhouse; right exit leads to road.*

AT RISE: *Stage is empty.* ZEKE *calls from offstage.*

ZEKE (*From offstage*): Brother Zack? You out there? (ZEKE *enters left. He is an elderly farmer, a typical old Yankee, in overalls and checked shirt.*) Now, where'd he go off to? I'd've swarn he were a-settin' right there a minute ago. (ZACK *enters right, carrying a wooden sign reading* TURN-PIKE—5 MILES.) Oh, there you are, Zack. Where you been?

ZACK: One o' them state highway crews went by a few minutes ago and tacked up another one o' them signs o' theirs.

ZEKE: Took it down, did you?

ZACK: Yep. Long as they keep a-puttin' 'em up on our property 'thout payin' rent, I intend to keep takin' 'em down.

ZEKE: What do you plan to do with it?

ZACK: I'll put it out in the barn, I reckon, 'long with the rest of 'em. Must be purt' near forty of 'em out there by this time, Zeke. Almost enough to put a new roof on the house.

ZEKE: It'll be the only roof in the village that says "five miles to the turnpike" forty times, I reckon.

ZACK (*Dryly*): Not after I paint it, it won't.

ZEKE: Wonder why the highway folks keep puttin' up signs. (*Sits in rocker*)

ZACK: Don't want folks to get lost, I reckon. (*Leans sign against side of straight chair and sits in other rocker*)

ZEKE: I think it's kind o' nice when folks get lost. Makes things a mite more sociable.

ZACK (*Looking off right*): By cracky, I think there's someone comin' now who just got lost. Leastways, a truck full of old furniture and a couple of fellers in city clothes just pulled off the road.

ZEKE: Must be a couple o' them antiquey dealers. Anythin' left out in the barn we kin sell 'em?

ZACK: Nope. Sold the last o' the milk cans last night. Got two dollars apiece for 'em. (*Smiling*) They were the oldest, rustiest milk cans in the county.

ZEKE: Reckon that's why you got two dollars apiece. If they'd been in good condition, they'd never fetch more'n a dollar seventy-five. (*Shakes head in wonder*) What in tarnation do city folks want with them old things?

ZACK (*Dryly*): At two dollars apiece, I ain't askin' any questions. (*Looks off right*) Yep, looks like we got a couple o' callers. (HARRIS *and* CARTER *enter from right. They are mopping their brows with their handkerchiefs.* ZEKE *and* ZACK *rock calmly.*)

HARRIS (*Calling*): Hey, there, old-timers—

ZEKE (*Slowly*): Howdy.

ZACK: Howdy.

HARRIS: Is this the road to the turnpike?

ZEKE: Nope. This here's the front yard of our farm. Ain't no road up here a-tall.

HARRIS (*Irritated*): No, no. (*Points off*) I mean that road down there.

ZACK: Then why didn't you say so, young feller?

CARTER: Let me handle this, Harris. You're always losing your temper. (*Turns to* ZEKE *and* ZACK) What my partner and I want to know is, where does the road go?

ZEKE: Don't go nowheres, far as I know. That right, Brother Zack?

ZACK: Yep. Allus been right where it is.

CARTER: No, no, no. What we mean is, can you give us directions? We're trying to get to New York.

ZEKE: Don't reckon I know how to get to New York.

CARTER: Well, then, can you tell us how to get to Hartford?

ZEKE: Don't reckon I know how to get to Hartford.

CARTER (*Irritated*): You don't know *much*, do you?

ZEKE (*Rocking, calmly*): Nope. But I ain't lost.

ZACK: You fellers antiquey dealers?

HARRIS (*Eagerly*): Why, yes, yes, we are. Anything you'd care to sell? Furniture? Silver?

CARTER (*Hopefully*): Milk cans?

ZACK: Nope. 'Fraid not. We're all cleaned out.

HARRIS (*Disappointed*): You're sure? Not even an old sampler?

ZEKE: *Did* have a sampler, but a feller talked me into selling it to him last week. Done by my Great-aunt Maudie, back in 1837. Sure hated to give it up. But the feller was awful persuasive. Way he talked, I just couldn't refuse him.

CARTER: Why? What did he say?

ZEKE: He said, "Five dollars."

HARRIS (*Outraged*): You let him buy an authentic 1837 sampler for five dollars? Why, those things are worth ten times that!

ZACK (*Opening his eyes wide*): Do tell. (*Innocently*) All that money for somethin' that just hangs on the wall?

HARRIS: You'd be surprised how valuable something that just hangs on the wall can be.

ZACK: Well, ain't that interestin', Brother Zeke?

ZEKE: Learn somethin' new every day, Brother Zack.

ZACK: You antiquey dealers sure are smart fellers.

CARTER (*To* HARRIS, *irritated*): Are you going to stand here making chitchat with a couple of hayseed farmers all day, Harris, or are we going to get back on the road?

HARRIS: Oh, yes. Can either of you gentlemen give us directions to the turnpike?

ZEKE (*Expansively*): Oh, is *that* what you wanted to know? Why, sure we kin! Fact is, we kin give you *two* sets o' directions, 'cause there's two ways o' gittin' there.

CARTER (*Smiling*): Just *one* way will be enough for us, thanks.

ZEKE (*Rising*): Let's see now. Well, you take your next right —that's Happy Valley Road. Go down there for about a mile and a quarter, and turn right when you see a barbed wire fence with some tiger lilies growin' on the outside of it. That'll be a dirt road. Now, you stay on that till you pass the third left. Turn there, go on for about six and a quarter miles—or maybe it's more like eight miles. Anyway, go right at the fork in the road, and go up there a piece till you pass the graveyard. When you get to the graveyard, you'll know you went too far, so turn around and go back a ways till you get to Gallows Lane. Take your second right, then your third left, then your second left. Go on to the fourth stop sign, just after the railroad crossing, turn left, go three and eight-tenths miles, turn right, and the turnpike'll be straight ahead of you. You can't miss it!

HARRIS (*Awestruck*): Did you get that, Carter?

CARTER (*Dazed*): Isn't there a shorter way?

ZEKE: Yep.

CARTER (*Exploding*): Then why didn't you tell me so in the first place?

ZEKE: You didn't ask.

HARRIS: I just don't understand it. What's wrong with the highway department around here? I'm sure there must be a turnpike sign *somewhere* in the neighborhood!

ZEKE (*Coughing*): Er, Brother Zack, isn't it about time you took that piece o' new lumber out to the barn?

ZACK: What's that? Oh! Oh, yeah, Brother Zeke, I reckon you're right. (*He picks up sign, turning it so* CARTER *and* HARRIS *can't read it, and carries it off right.*)

CARTER: Now, about that shortcut . . .

ZEKE: Well, now, come to think of it, I've got a map o' the shortcut. Yep, a beautiful state highway map that shows just how to git to the turnpike from here.

HARRIS (*Happily*): That's marvelous! Could we look at it?

ZEKE: Well, now, I don't know. You see, I got it taped up on the wall in my bedroom. There's a water spot in the wallpaper, and that map sure comes in handy for coverin' it up.

CARTER (*Exasperated*): Well, surely you can let us take a *look* at it!

ZEKE: Maybe I could be *persuaded* to. . . .

CARTER (*Getting the message*): You sure don't miss a trick, do you? All right, I'll give you a dollar for the map.

ZEKE: Five dollars.

CARTER (*Exploding*): Five dollars for a piece of paper you're using to cover up a stain in your wallpaper? That's outrageous!

ZEKE (*Dryly*): You'd be surprised how valuable somethin' that just hangs on the wall can be.

HARRIS (*Exasperated*): Oh, give the man five dollars, Carter, so we can find our way out of here. (*Paces about*)

CARTER (*Grimly*): All right, then. Five dollars for the map.

ZEKE (*Holding out his hand*): In advance, o' course. (CARTER, *furious, hands bill to* ZEKE, *who takes it and exits left.* HARRIS *watches him until he is out of sight, then turns to* CARTER.)

HARRIS (*In low, urgent voice*): Carter!

CARTER: What is it?

HARRIS (*Eagerly*): While you and that hayseed were talking, I happened to notice something. Look at that chair—the one the cat's sleeping in.

CARTER (*Doing a double take*): Good grief! Is it—is it—?

HARRIS: Yes! An authentic Shepplewhite-Fitchcock chair!

CARTER: And in perfect condition! Why—do you know what that chair is worth?

HARRIS: I know the Metropolitan Museum paid sixteen thousand dollars for one that wasn't nearly as good!

CARTER: Do you think these old farmers know what they've got here?

HARRIS (*Gloatingly*): Not a chance! Didn't he say he had nothing of any value to sell?

CARTER: Offer him fifty bucks for it. He'll jump at it!

HARRIS: No, no, no! That'd be too obvious. If I offer him money for the chair, he'll smell a rat, and that'll push the price up.

CARTER: But if you don't offer him money—

HARRIS (*Tapping his head; shrewdly*): Psychology, Carter.

Psychology. You've got to use your head when you're dealing with these simple peasant types. Just leave it to me.

ZACK (*Re-entering, right*): You fellers still here? Where's Brother Zeke?

HARRIS: Oh, he went into the house to get us a map. And while he's been gone, my partner and I have been admiring your cat here, haven't we, Carter?

CARTER (*Blankly*): Cat?

HARRIS (*Expansively*): Yes, that darling little kitty-cat sleeping on that rickety old good-for-nothing broken-down chair.

CARTER (*Understanding*): Oh, *that* cat.

HARRIS: And we were wondering, my partner and I, whether you'd consider selling her. We think that is the most beautiful little kitty-cat we've ever seen. We just must have her, mustn't we, Carter?

CARTER: Oh, yes. Yes!

ZACK: Well, I reckon you'll have to ask Brother Zeke about that. It's his cat.

ZEKE (*Entering left with map*): Someone mention my name? (*To* CARTER) Here's your map, young feller. (*Gives it to* CARTER)

ZACK: Seems these fellers are interested in buyin' your cat, Zeke.

ZEKE (*Horrified*): What? Sell old Puss-Cat? Puss-Cat, that's been in the family for fifteen years? Why, Puss is like our own flesh and blood. We couldn't live without her. (*Cynically*) How much'll you give?

HARRIS (*Hopefully*): Ten dollars?

ZEKE (*Firmly*): Fifteen.

HARRIS: Ten-fifty.

ZACK (*In auctioneer's tones*): I have ten-fifty, ten-fifty. Who'll say eleven?

CARTER (*Eagerly*): Eleven!

ZACK: Eleven! Do I hear twelve? Twelve? Will anyone bid twelve?

HARRIS: Twelve!

ZACK (*Slapping his hands together*): Sold! To the sucker in the—I mean, the gentleman in the blue suit, for twelve dollars. (ZEKE *holds out his hand.* HARRIS *takes out wallet, counts out bills, hands them to* ZEKE. ZACK *picks up sleeping cat and places it in* HARRIS's *arms.*)

ZEKE: Just twelve dollars for old Puss-Cat! You antiquey dealers sure are right smart fellers!

HARRIS (*Pretending to get a sudden thought*): Say! This kitty-cat looked so peaceful sleeping on that rickety old good-for-nothing broken-down chair, I'm *sure* she'd want it to go with her to her new home. I'll give you fifty cents for the chair. (*Casually*) Not that it's worth anything, of course, but just to make Puss-Cat happy.

ZEKE: Nope. No sale.

HARRIS (*Taken aback*): I suppose I shouldn't, but—well, all right, I'll give you a dollar. Only to make Puss-Cat happy.

ZEKE: Nope.

HARRIS: Two dollars?

CARTER: Five dollars?

HARRIS: Ten dollars?

ZEKE (*Still shaking his head*): Sorry, but that chair ain't for sale a-tall. Not at any price.

HARRIS (*Disgusted*): Why not?

ZEKE: That's my lucky chair. Every antiquey dealer that stops here buys a cat off that chair for at least ten dollars. Why, yours is the third cat I've sold this week. (*He goes off left, returns at once with another cat, and puts it on chair.*) There, there, kitty. Take a nice nap while you can. The way things are goin', you'll be sold to a new owner inside o' fifteen minutes!

CARTER (*To* HARRIS, *in disgust*): You and your psychology! You're now the proud owner of a twelve-dollar alley cat. Come on, let's get out of here before you decide to buy another one. (*They start off.*)

ZEKE (*Rocking gently in his chair*): So long, strangers! Good o' you to drop in.

ZACK (*Likewise*): Yep, you be sure an' come see us again some time, hear?

HARRIS (*Sarcastically, as he and* CARTER *exit*): Yes, we'll do that.

ZEKE: Hm-m. They didn't seem too friendly, did they, Brother Zack?

ZACK: Nope, can't say as they did. Well, maybe the next bunch that stops'll be nicer.

ZEKE (*Looking off right*): I hear an engine now. Think it's some more right smart antiquey fellers lookin' for the turnpike?

ZACK (*Rising and looking off*): Nope. I'll be danged if it ain't the state highway crew, come to put up another sign!

ZEKE (*Rocking slowly*): Well, ain't they the friendly ones? After the roof gets finished, we can start building us a new barn! (*He and* ZACK *chuckle contentedly and continue rocking slowly. Curtain*)

THE END

The Three Swine
of Most Small Stature

An old favorite goes Oriental

Characters

STAGE MANAGER   NUMBER THREE PIG
NUMBER ONE PIG   WON TON WOLF
NUMBER TWO PIG

BEFORE RISE: *A gong sounds offstage.* STAGE MANAGER *steps out from between the curtains and bows low to audience.* NOTE: *The acting should be highly stylized, with the actors pantomiming most of the action in pseudo-Oriental fashion.*

STAGE MANAGER: O most revered audience, welcome to Imperial Theater of the Orient. I, Oriental Stage Manager, beg your humble attention. Wish to have your permission to introduce play. Wish to introduce play even *without* your permission, since actors have been rehearsing for a week. Play tells very ancient and honorable legend: legend of the Three Swine of Most Small Stature. Called in translation, "The Three Little Pigs." Perhaps you have read legend already, in which case, feel free to nap during performance. However, must warn you that legend in English not so beautiful as legend in Chinese. In Chinese is very symbolic . . . very aesthetic. Also very hard to understand if you don't speak Chinese. (*Gong sounds offstage.*) Ah, so! Signal means, "Let's get this show on the road." (*Bows*) The Three Swine of Most Small Stature. (*He claps his hands and the curtains open.*)

* * *

SETTING: *Bare stage. A cut-out tree stands at one side.*

AT RISE: *The three* PIGS *are dancing and skipping about.*

STAGE MANAGER: Behold! A woodland glade in ancient China. Notice: only one tree for scenery. One tree suggests entire woodland. Very symbolic. Very aesthetic. (*Claps hands.* PIGS *stop frolicking and stand in line.*) Beg to introduce chief characters. (PIGS *step forward and bow as their names are called.*) Number One Pig. (*He bows.*) Number Two Pig. (*He bows.*) Number Three Pig. (*He bows.*) Play has one other character. We will introduce him later. For one thing, wish to build suspense. For another thing, he takes a long time to get into his costume. (*The gong sounds.*) Signal! Signal means: "Let play begin!" (STAGE MANAGER *kneels at side of stage.*)

NUMBER ONE PIG: Oink!

NUMBER TWO PIG: Oink!

NUMBER THREE PIG: Oink!

NUMBER ONE PIG: Brother pigs, what a happy life we live here in ancient China.

NUMBER TWO PIG: You have spoken wisely, Number One Pig. Ours is the most carefree existence.

NUMBER THREE PIG: Nothing to do but sing and play, all day long.

NUMBER ONE PIG: Yes, fun is good. But when I spoke of

pleasure, I meant also the pleasure of work. The pleasure of going to school. The pleasure of meeting challenges and pursuing honest toil.

NUMBER TWO PIG: What a party-pooper you are, Number One Pig. Number Three Pig and I don't believe in all that work stuff.

NUMBER THREE PIG: Naw, we just want to dance and sing and have a good time all day long.

NUMBER ONE PIG: Foolish, foolish pigs! Listen to me, your elder brother. All play and no work make for great unhappiness.

NUMBER TWO PIG: Says who?

NUMBER ONE PIG: Old saying of Confucius.

NUMBER TWO PIG (*Disgusted*): Ah, you and your high-flown ideas! Just because you went to college, you're always showing off.

NUMBER THREE PIG: You used to be a regular guy, Number One Pig. But ever since you took your Ph.D. in Pig Latin, have you been a grouch!

NUMBER ONE PIG: You may scoff at me now, my brothers. But one day you will see I am right.

STAGE MANAGER (*Rising, addressing audience*): Number One Pig wasn't exaggerating. He knew that summer could not last forever. Behold: Winter! (*He hangs a giant snowflake cutout on the tree.*) Cold, cold, cold winter—the worst winter in the history of China. Notice: Only one snowflake for scenery. One snowflake meant to suggest all of winter. Very symbolic. Very aesthetic.

NUMBER THREE PIG: Also very cheap.

STAGE MANAGER: Now came the time to work, just as Number One Pig had predicted.

NUMBER ONE PIG: Oink!

NUMBER TWO PIG: Oink!

NUMBER THREE PIG: Oink!

NUMBER ONE PIG: My brothers, it is winter. We can no longer live out of doors. I think it is time to build a pagoda.

NUMBER TWO PIG (*Sarcastically*): It's really terrific to have a college graduate in the family. It's been snowing for a month now, and it's finally dawned on him to build us a house.

NUMBER THREE PIG: I was wondering when you were going to get around to it, Number One Pig.

NUMBER ONE PIG (*Smugly*): But, my brothers, I am not going to build *us* a house. I am going to build *me* a house. You must build houses for yourselves.

NUMBER TWO PIG: Big deal. I guess we can build as good a house as you can if we want to.

NUMBER ONE PIG: We shall see. What will you build your house of, Number Three Pig?

NUMBER THREE PIG: I shall build my house of tatami mats. I know where I can get a real buy on good straw tatami mats, imported from Japan.

NUMBER ONE PIG: If I may say so, esteemed, honorable, and revered brother, it's a stupid idea. I might call it tatami-rot!

NUMBER TWO PIG and NUMBER THREE PIG (*Groaning in unison*): Oink!

NUMBER ONE PIG: And what will you build your house of, Number Two Pig?

NUMBER TWO PIG: I shall build my house of chopsticks. I can get second-hand chopsticks free down at the Chinese restaurant.

NUMBER ONE PIG: House of straw! House of sticks! Is terrible architecture.

NUMBER TWO PIG (*Wagging his finger; brightly*): But is symbolic!

NUMBER THREE PIG (*Likewise*): Is aesthetic!

NUMBER ONE PIG (*Proudly*): I shall build *my* house of bricks.

NUMBER TWO PIG: Bricks! But bricks cost a fortune!

NUMBER THREE PIG: Where would you get the money?

NUMBER ONE PIG: Have been making regular deposits at the Piggy Bank. You forget: I am college graduate. I really know how to bring home the bacon.

NUMBER TWO PIG *and* NUMBER THREE PIG (*Groaning in unison*): Oink!

STAGE MANAGER (*Rising*): And so, the Three Swine of Most Small Stature set to work to build themselves the best pagodas they could manage. (PIGS *pantomime building houses.*) Number One Pig built his house of bricks, while Number Two Pig built his of chopsticks and Number Three Pig used tatami. And when the pagodas were finished, how pleased the pigs were.

NUMBER ONE PIG: Oink!

NUMBER TWO PIG: Oink!

NUMBER THREE PIG: Oink!

STAGE MANAGER: Story now becomes complicated. Is late one night. Each pig sits in his own pagoda. No scenery for night. No scenery for pagodas. Audience must use imagination. We blew our budget on the snowflake. Suddenly, out of the woods comes dark, mysterious figure. (WON TON WOLF *enters and slinks around at back of stage.*) Wicked creature. Evil creature. Hush! Plot thickens! (WOLF *pretends to knock on door of straw house by stamping his foot on the stage as he raps his hand in the air.*)

WOLF: O, most revered Number Three Pig, I beg you to give me admittance to your snug little pagoda.

NUMBER THREE PIG: Who is that knocking on my door?

WOLF: It is I, your humble friend and neighbor, Won Ton Wolf. Let me in, let me in!

NUMBER THREE PIG: Not by the hair of my Chinny Chin-Chin.

WOLF (*Perplexed*): What the heck is a Chinny Chin-Chin?

NUMBER THREE PIG: Oh. Is my girlfriend. Her name is Chin-Chin. "Chinny" is her nickname.

WOLF (*Still perplexed*): Well, what on earth does her hair have to do with it?

NUMBER THREE PIG: Her hair is her most beautiful feature. It is what caused me to fall in love with her. (*Sings*) "I dream of Chinny with the light brown hair. . . ."

WOLF (*Disgusted*): What is this, Chinese amateur night? Let me in, I say!

NUMBER THREE PIG: Never!

WOLF: Then I'll huff and I'll puff and I'll blow your house in!

NUMBER THREE PIG: And then what will you do?

WOLF (*Laughing wickedly*): I'll turn you into pork chow mein!

STAGE MANAGER (*As WOLF huffs and puffs*): So Wolf huffed. Wolf puffed. Son of Confucius! Wolf blew house in! (NUMBER THREE PIG *falls over*.) Fortunately, Pig escaped to pagoda of Number Two Pig. (NUMBER THREE PIG *runs over to* NUMBER TWO PIG.)

NUMBER THREE PIG: Listen, brother, I'm in big trouble. May I spend the night with you?

NUMBER TWO PIG: Of course. But what happened? (WOLF *knocks at door of second house*.)

NUMBER THREE PIG: Never mind. I think it's about to happen again.

WOLF: O, most noble and esteemed Number Two Pig, let me in, let me in.

NUMBER TWO PIG (*To* NUMBER THREE PIG): Who can that be?

NUMBER THREE PIG (*Dryly*): Well, it ain't Madame Butterfly.

NUMBER TWO PIG (*Dramatically*): You mean—?

NUMBER THREE PIG (*Nodding*): Yep. Won Ton Wolf.

NUMBER TWO PIG (*To* WOLF): You've got to be kidding, O most feared and vicious wolf. Never will I let you in, not by the hair of my brother's Chinny Chin-Chin. (*Pause*) Aren't you going to ask me what a Chinny Chin-Chin is?

WOLF: Forget it. I've been that route already. Are you going to open up or do I go into my huff-and-puff stuff?

NUMBER TWO PIG: What will you do if I let you in?

WOLF: I'll turn you into Barbecued Spare Ribs with Sesame Soy Sauce.

STAGE MANAGER (*As* WOLF *huffs*): Again, Wolf huffed. Wolf puffed. Again, success. (NUMBER TWO *and* NUMBER THREE PIGS *fall over*.) Sky looked as if it was raining chopsticks. Just in nick of time, Number Two Pig and Number Three Pig made it to pagoda of Number One Pig. (*They race over to* NUMBER ONE PIG.)

NUMBER ONE PIG: O my most honorable brothers, to what do I owe the esteemed pleasure of this unexpected visit?

NUMBER TWO PIG: It's Won Ton Wolf.

NUMBER THREE PIG: He's after us!

NUMBER ONE PIG (*Smugly*): Why did you not seek refuge in your own pagodas?

NUMBER THREE PIG: All right, don't rub it in. That tatami of mine just shriveled to bits. It never pays to buy cheap foreign merchandise.

NUMBER TWO PIG: And my chopsticks weren't much use, either. You were very clever, Number One Pig, to build your house of bricks.

NUMBER ONE PIG (*Modestly*): Well, to tell the truth, I

didn't get the idea by myself. Read it in a fortune cookie.

NUMBER THREE PIG: Who cares how you got the idea! Will you let us stay with you?

NUMBER ONE PIG: Do you think I'd throw my esteemed brothers into the cold, and keep all this warmth and safety for myself? What do you take me for—a pig?

STAGE MANAGER: So the Three Swine of Most Small Stature waited in their safe brick pagoda for the arrival of their enemy. He was not long in showing up.

WOLF (*Pretending to knock*): O, most esteemed Number One Pig, let me in, let me in.

THREE PIGS (*In unison, singing*): "I dream of Chinny with the light brown hair. . . ."

WOLF (*Angrily*): Oh, you're pulling that on me, are you? O.K., wise guys, prepare yourselves for some huffing and puffing that'll blow you all into won ton soup!

STAGE MANAGER (*As WOLF huffs*): Wolf huffed. Wolf puffed. But, lo! Brick pagoda did not give way. Number One Pig had built too strongly. Pigs were safe! Wolf was outfoxed!

WOLF (*To STAGE MANAGER*): Oh, yeah? Well, there's more than one way to skin a kumquat. I have a sneaky plan that will let me get into that pagoda even if it *is* made of bricks.

STAGE MANAGER: What's your plan?

WOLF (*Triumphantly*): I'll climb up on the roof and drop down the chimney! Just wait'll I get a ladder. (WOLF *exits. Gong is heard.* STAGE MANAGER *turns to audience.*)

STAGE MANAGER: O most revered audience, it would be a pleasure to show you outcome of devious plan of Won Ton Wolf. However, is impossible in our humble theater. Not enough money to show roof. Not enough money to show chimney. Not even enough money for symbolic, aesthetic ladder. Besides, actor playing Wolf afraid of heights. However, I can tell you how story ended. Number One Pig said:

NUMBER ONE PIG: O, my brothers, after your adventure in the cold, wintry night, I'll bet you'd like a cup of nice hot Formosa Oolong tea. I will just set a giant cauldron of water—which I happen to have lying about the house —in the fireplace and let it come to a boil.

NUMBER TWO PIG: You really shouldn't bother, Number One Pig.

NUMBER THREE PIG: Yes, why go to all that trouble?

NUMBER ONE PIG: Well, you never can tell. Someone may be dropping in.

STAGE MANAGER: And so, clever Number One Pig came up with stratagem that cooked Wolf's goose. But in any case, Wolf would have met sad fate, and story would have had happy ending. For as it is written in ancient, honorable Chinese proverb, "He who drops down Oriental chimney comes down with case of Hong Kong flue." Get it? Flue? (*Bows low. Blackout and quick curtain*)

THE END

Try Data-Date!

Match-making by computer

Characters

CHARLIE COOL, *manager of Data-Date*
JIM JETSET, *his assistant*
HAROLD FENDEL, *a reluctant customer*
PHIL, *the friendly salesman*
THE DATE

SETTING: *The Office of Data-Date, a computer dating firm. A desk and three chairs are at one side. Up center is the computer, an enormous cardboard box large enough to conceal an actor, and covered with knobs, dials, switches, reels of tape, gears, lights, etc. A door is cut into one part of the front.* THE DATE *is inside computer. This skit may be played before the curtain.*

AT RISE: CHARLIE *is sitting at desk, making a list.* JIM *relaxes in chair. They are high-pressure, hard-boiled con-man types.*

CHARLIE (*As he writes*): Let's see now. A yacht . . . a couple of swimming pools . . . an apartment in Paris . . .

JIM: What are you doing, Charlie?

CHARLIE: I'm making a list of all the things I'm going to buy with my fortune.

JIM: Fortune? What fortune?

CHARLIE: It's only a matter of time, my friend. With our super-duper dating service, we're going to be rolling in money any day now.

JIM (*Pointing to computer*): You really think that thing is going to make us a fortune?

CHARLIE (*Going to computer protectively*): Please! Do not refer to it as "that thing." Why, this machine is the greatest invention since the chicken. No more does mankind have to struggle in the darkness, trusting to luck, instinct, and a helpful mother to find the girl of his dreams. Now, it's the computer to the rescue! You feed the machine the data on your ideal dreamboat, and presto! There she is. I tell you, Jim, this Data-Date service of ours is going to make us rich, rich, rich!

JIM (*Skeptically*): You really think we're going to make it?

CHARLIE (*Grandly*): How can we miss? With your talent and my brains—(*Thinks about that a second, then shakes his head*) I mean, with my talent and your brains —(*Thinks, shakes head again*) I mean, with *my* talent and *my* brains, we're going to clean up!

JIM: Then how come we don't have any customers yet?

CHARLIE: Patience, patience, my friend. I have Phil the friendly salesman out this very minute, drumming up trade. And what a salesman! Jim, you should see that guy work. He's smooth. He's sophisticated. He uses the soft-sell approach.

HAROLD (*Shouting, from offstage*): Put me down! Put me down!

CHARLIE: I do believe he's coming now, with our first customer. (PHIL *enters, propelling* HAROLD *along.* PHIL *has one of* HAROLD's *arms twisted behind his back, and the other arm wrapped around his neck.* PHIL *is a brawny type.*)

HAROLD: Let me go! Let me go!

PHIL (*To* CHARLIE): Morning, boss. I've brought you a customer.

CHARLIE: Good, good. See what I mean, Jim?

JIM: Yeah. Smooth. Sophisticated. Soft sell.

PHIL: What shall I do with him, boss?

CHARLIE: You can let him go now. (PHIL *releases* HAROLD, *who is sputtering and trying to regain his dignity.*)

HAROLD: This is an outrage! Wait till I tell my congressman about this!

PHIL: You want me to go out and find another customer, boss?

CHARLIE: Better wait outside the door, Phil—just in case *this* one tries to get away.

PHIL: O.K., boss. (*He goes out.*)

CHARLIE (*To* HAROLD): Welcome to Data-Date, sir, your friendly local computer Cupid. And what can we do for you?

HAROLD (*Frostily*): You can let me out of here, that's what you can do.

CHARLIE (*To* JIM): He's just like all the rest, Jim—can't wait to get in here, but then he turns a little shy. (*To* HAROLD) Now, why don't you just sit down and relax while I tell you how our service works.

HAROLD: I don't want to relax. I want to leave.

CHARLIE (*Elaborately polite*): Well, in that case, sir, why don't you just leave? The door is open (HAROLD *starts for the door.*) . . . and Phil the friendly salesman is standing right outside.

HAROLD (*Stopping in his tracks*): On second thought, I want to relax. (*He sits.*)

CHARLIE: Ah, you won't regret it. Will he, Jim?

JIM: No, sir, you won't regret it. Why, aren't you excited to be taking part in one of the greatest technological miracles of the century? You're a pioneer! An adventurer! A trail-blazer through the mists of the future!

HAROLD (*Blankly*): I am?

CHARLIE: Why, compared with the adventure you are about to undergo, a trip to the moon is like a walk around the block by a six-year-old.

HAROLD (*Frightened*): You're not getting *me* to take part in any scientific experiments! Let me out of here! (*Jumps up, starts out*)

CHARLIE (*Pointedly*): Give my regards to Phil the friendly salesman in the hall.

HAROLD (*Resignedly*): O.K., O.K. Now what's this all about? (*Sits again*)

JIM: Wouldn't you like to be one of history's immortal lovers?

HAROLD: Huh?

CHARLIE: With the girl of your dreams, you could become famous forever. Like Romeo and Juliet.

JIM: Like Tristan and Isolde.

HAROLD (*Trying to grasp the idea*): Like Mutt and Jeff?

CHARLIE: No, no. Like Lancelot and Guinevere.

JIM: Like Abelard and Heloise.

CHARLIE: Like Marvin and Sylvia.

HAROLD: Who are Marvin and Sylvia?

CHARLIE: Marvin Jenks and Sylvia Applebaum. They've been going steady since second grade.

JIM (*Enthusiastically*): Just fill out our friendly little 803-part questionnaire in triplicate, and in an instant, Data-Date will provide you with the girl of your dreams.

HAROLD: But I already *have* the girl of my dreams. I'm going with Myrna Flynn.

CHARLIE: Say, I know her! Oh, she's a nice girl all right—but for a guy like *you*, well . . .

HAROLD: What about a guy like me?

CHARLIE: You're smooth—brilliant—handsome!

JIM: Yeah. You're a sharpie—a smoothie—a real winner! You deserve the best there is!

CHARLIE: Jim is right. Myrna's O.K.—but you should be going with a princess—a movie star—an English teacher.

HAROLD: I—I should?

CHARLIE: Would I lie? To you? A guy I love like my own brother? By the way—what's your name?

HAROLD: Harold Fendel.

CHARLIE (*Rubbing his hands together*): Harold, let's get down to business. It's really very simple—only two little items to take care of. Item number one: Our fee.

HAROLD: Fee?

CHARLIE: Seventy-five dollars.

JIM: Cash.

CHARLIE: In advance.

HAROLD: But—but I don't have seventy-five dollars.

CHARLIE (*Easily*): Oh, that's our *regular* fee. But today—for one time only—we have a special introductory offer. Twenty-seven fifty.

HAROLD (*Shaking head, rising to go*): Oh, I'm afraid twenty-seven fifty . . .

JIM (*Interrupting quickly*): How about a buck and a quarter?

HAROLD (*Happily*): Now that's more like it.

CHARLIE (*Pinching his cheek, playfully*): Say, kid, you sure know how to bargain! But I like you, I like you. You're smooth—you're suave—

JIM (*Dryly*): Enough with the smooth, Charlie. We gave him that line already.

CHARLIE: O.K. Item number two: Our confidential, comprehensive, in-depth, analytical, psychological question-naire. (*Pulls from desk a large telephone directory cov-ered with plain paper and hands it to* HAROLD) Now if you'll just fill this out in triplicate, we'll feed it to the computer, and presto! You will have the girl of your dreams.

HAROLD: But—but I don't have time to fill out all of that.

JIM: Don't worry about that, my friend. Charlie and I are ready for every emergency.

CHARLIE: Right! In cases like yours, we switch to the short form. Three or four simple questions, and that's it.

HAROLD: But how can you find me the girl of my dreams with only three or four questions?

JIM (*Dryly*): You never had a nightmare?

CHARLIE (*Thrusting card and pencil at him*): Go to it, Harold, my friend. And don't be nervous. (*As* HAROLD *fills out card,* JIM *and* CHARLIE *joyfully shake hands with each other behind his back.* HAROLD *looks up from card.*)

HAROLD: How do you spell "Monopoly"?

CHARLIE: What?

HAROLD: The card says to write down what you like to do on a date. I like to play Monopoly.

CHARLIE (*Snatching card from him*): That's O.K., Harold, my boy. I'm sure you've already put down all the crucial information. (*Professionally*) Now, we just feed the card into the machine—thusly (*Inserts card into computer*) . . . Press the go button—thusly . . . and let 'er rip! (*Clanking and whirring noises come from machine. If desired, tapes and gears can turn, etc.*)

JIM (*Triumphantly, when machine stops*): And now—the moment of truth!

CHARLIE (*Expansively*): Knock upon the door, my good Harold, and see what the computer hath wrought on your behalf.

HAROLD (*Going to door on computer, knocking timidly*):
Are you there, O girl of my dreams? (*From behind the
door comes the sound of a dog barking.*)

JIM (*Horrified*): Something's gone wrong!

CHARLIE (*Quickly*): Ah! I see at once what it is. Just be patient, Harold, my boy, and I'll have everything straightened out in a jiffy. I left the frammis plug hooked into
the zilch sprocket, before engaging the differential sprang
hook. (*Makes adjustments on machine*) There! That's
more like it. Now, let's try it again.

HAROLD (*Apprehensively*): You're—you're sure this thing
is going to work?

CHARLIE: I guarantee you, Harold, that when that door
opens and you see the date the machine has picked out
for you, you won't believe your eyes!

JIM: All set, Charlie?

CHARLIE: Let 'er rip! (JIM *starts machine, which clanks and
whirs, etc., as before, then stops.*) O.K., Harold, she's all
yours!

HAROLD (*Calling, timidly*): Come out, come out, whoever
you are! (*Door of computer opens, and* THE DATE, *a
gorilla, walks out with arms extended.* HAROLD *faints in
shock, as* JIM *and* CHARLIE *look on in horror. Blackout.*)

THE END

The Once and Future Frog

Can this marriage be saved?

Characters

PRINCESS ANGELA   QUEEN IMOGEN
PRINCE FREDERICK   KING MARMADUKE

SETTING: *A room in King Marmaduke's castle. In one wall, there is a large, low open window. Next to it there is a low chest, and near that, a stool. Up center is a door to the rest of the castle. At left stand a writing desk and chair. Several other chairs stand left and right.*

AT RISE: PRINCESS ANGELA *is seated at the desk, addressing wedding invitations.* PRINCE FREDERICK, *dressed all in green, is sitting across room staring into space. He holds a flyswatter. Every so often he spots a fly, follows it with his eyes, and then suddenly leaps up and swats it.*

ANGELA (*As she writes address*): Prince Charming and Princess Snow White. Post Office Box 247, Fairyland. (*Takes another envelope*) Prince Charming and Princess Cinderella . . . (*Looks up*) Fred, how many l's in Cinderella? (FRED *jumps up and swats at a fly on wall.*)
FRED (*Angrily*): Missed!
ANGELA: Fred, I asked you a question.
FRED (*Blankly*): Huh?

ANGELA: Oh, never mind. Three l's ought to be enough. (*Writes*) The Crystal Castle, Route Three, Fairyland. (*Takes another envelope.*) Prince Charming and Princess Rapunzel . . .

FRED: Don't princes around here have any names except Charming?

ANGELA: One or two. But the Charmings are probably the biggest royal family in Fairyland—and they have nothing but sons. It's sort of a tradition with them. Sooner or later, everyone who's anyone marries one of the Charming boys.

FRED: Are *you* going to marry one of them?

ANGELA (*Puzzled*): Me? Of course not, darling. I'm marrying *you*.

FRED: Oh, that's right. I keep forgetting.

ANGELA: At least, I am if I ever get all these wedding invitations addressed. (FRED *sees a fly land on the desk. He leaps toward it, swats at it, and scatters the invitations.*)

FRED (*Triumphantly*): Got it!

ANGELA (*Collecting invitations*): Fred, what *is* the matter with you? How can I ever get the invitations finished if you're going to keep interrupting me with your flyswatter?

FRED: I—I can't help it, Angela. I know it annoys you, but it's just an irresistible impulse I have. I see a fly, and—wham! I can't sit still until I've swatted it.

ANGELA: Well, do try to control yourself. Flies are part of your past. You have to make an effort to forget about that sort of thing. Now, where's your guest list for the wedding?

FRED (*Ashamed*): I—I haven't made it up yet.

ANGELA: I wish you would. The wedding's only three weeks away, and—

FRED: Angela . . . Angela, I want to talk to you about the wedding.

ANGELA (*Apprehensive*): What is it, Fred? You sound so serious.

FRED: Angela . . . Angela, I've been thinking. (*With difficulty*) I wonder if we aren't being a little—well, a little impetuous.

ANGELA: Impetuous? We've known each other for a whole day and a half, haven't we? What's impetuous about that?

FRED (*Uncomfortably*): Well, it just seems to me that we're being a bit hasty. I mean, I just don't think that my ability to fetch a golden ball out of a well is a sufficiently solid basis for something as serious as marriage.

ANGELA (*Lightly*): Oh, is that what's worrying you? My goodness, Frederick, I'm not marrying you because you fetched the golden ball.

FRED (*Hopefully*): You're not?

ANGELA: Of course not! I'm marrying you because I broke the spell you were under.

FRED (*Downcast again*): Oh.

ANGELA (*Explaining patiently*): A princess *always* marries a prince when she breaks the spell he's been under. And vice versa. What better test could there be that two people were made for each other?

FRED (*Unhappily*): But how can a marriage work out when two people don't have anything in common?

ANGELA: Look at Prince Charming and Cinderella. He only married her because she had a tiny foot—and yet they lived happily ever after. At least they have so far. Look at King Florizel and Queen Brangaene. Talk about differences in background! He grew up in the lap of luxury, and she was just a simple farm girl. But she began spinning straw into gold, and—poof! Instant romance! Look at Prince Charming and Sleeping Beauty. Look at King Thrushbeard and Queen Katharina.

FRED (*Morosely*): Look at Mr. Owl and Miss Pussycat.

ANGELA: Who on earth are Mr. Owl and Miss Pussycat?

FRED: Oh, they're just some people I happen to know. When *they* got married, all they had in common was joint ownership of a beautiful pea-green boat. Well, believe me, it wasn't enough to make the marriage work. Fights, quarrels, arguments all the time. You should have seen the way the fur and feathers flew!

ANGELA (*Patiently*): But, Fred, those are animals. With people, it's different.

FRED: But we're *not* people, Angela. I mean, *I'm* not. Not really.

ANGELA (*Soothingly*): Of course you are, Fred. You're a prince.

FRED: But just the other day I was a frog.

ANGELA: I know, darling. That was because you were under a spell. You were a prince who was turned into a frog.

FRED (*Shaking his head unhappily*): Uh-uh.

ANGELA: What do you mean?

FRED (*Blurting it out*): Oh, Angela, you might as well know the truth. I wasn't a prince who was turned into a frog. I'm a frog who's been turned into a prince.

ANGELA (*Confused*): I don't understand, Fred, I—(QUEEN IMOGEN *and* KING MARMADUKE *enter.*)

QUEEN (*Interrupting, happily*): Oh, Angela, darling, I've just been talking to the caterers, and we have the most wonderful ideas for the reception! There's going to be a centerpiece shaped like a swan, all made out of chopped liver. Then we're going to have platters of cold cuts— hummingbird tongues, peacock drumsticks, frogs' legs . . .

FRED: Oh! How can you!

QUEEN (*Embarrassed*): Oh! Oh, my goodness, Frederick, I wasn't thinking! Of *course* we won't have frog—those things. I'll tell you what! We'll leave the whole menu up to you. You decide what should be served.

FRED: Well, I've always kind of liked earthworms.

QUEEN (*Shuddering*): Earthworms! You can't be serious!

ANGELA: Oh, don't pay any attention to him, Mother. He's just a little upset.

KING: Upset? What's there to be upset about? You're marrying the prettiest little princess in all of Fairyland, aren't you?

FRED (*Bravely*): Sir—could I speak with you for a minute? I mean seriously—man to frog.

KING: Sure, Frederick. What's on your mind?

FRED: Well . . . there seems to be a misunderstanding. You all seem to think that I'm a prince. But I'm not a prince. I'm a frog.

QUEEN: You mean you *were* a frog. But the spell has been broken, and all that is past. Don't give it another thought.

KING: We understand these things, Frederick. You sow a few wild oats, some witch gets mad at you, and she turns you into a frog. Boys will be boys. Why, when I was your age, you know what I was? I was a beast.

QUEEN (*Simpering*): And I was a beauty!

KING: And you still are, my dear. You still are.

FRED: No, no, no. How can I make you understand? I'm a frog—a real frog. That's the way I was born. The only reason you think I'm a prince is that I'm under a spell.

QUEEN (*With sudden realization*): You mean—you're not an enchanted prince?

FRED (*Miserably*): Uh-uh. I'm an enchanted frog. I'm only a prince temporarily, until the spell is broken. But as soon as somebody manages to break the spell—splash! It's back to the frog pond for yours truly.

KING: But this is preposterous! Why would anybody turn a frog into a prince?

FRED: Well, I hate to admit it, but I did a bad thing.

ANGELA: Oh, I can't believe that, Frederick. Sweet, kind, good, noble you? What bad thing could you have done?

FRED: Well, it was like this. The other day you dropped your golden ball into the well, remember?

ANGELA: Yes. And you brought it back to me.

FRED: That's where I made my mistake. You see, there's a witch who lives in the bottom of the well, and she wanted to keep the golden ball.

KING (*Knowingly*): You should have let her. You don't want to go fooling around with witches, my boy.

FRED (*Urgently*): But I couldn't let the ball stay in the well. We frogs are deeply concerned about water pollution— and we can't put up with minerals in the water. I felt I just had to get that golden ball out of there. So I hopped up on land with it—and that's when the witch put the spell on me. She was so angry that she turned me into a prince.

ANGELA (*Sympathetically*): No wonder all this wedding talk made you so uncomfortable.

FRED (*Nodding*): I've felt like a frog out of water the whole time.

KING: But see here, Frederick—

FRED: Oh, call me Croaker, please. That's my real name.

KING: Do you mean to say you aren't going to marry Angela?

FRED: I don't really see how I can, do you? Nothing personal, Angela—but you do understand my predicament, don't you?

ANGELA (*Wiping a tear from her eye*): Oh, yes, I do, Fred
—I mean, Croaker.

QUEEN: Did the witch tell you what it would take to break
the enchantment? (*To* KING) They're morally obligated
to do that, you know. I think it's even written into their
contracts.

FRED: I'm not sure. I *think* she said something about the
spell being over when I found a girl who wasn't afraid of
warts. I'm not sure, though. It was tough to understand
—she was speaking under water.

KING: Well, Angela? Are *you* afraid of warts?

ANGELA (*Grimacing in distaste*): Oh, Daddy, I think they're
awful!

FRED (*With a sigh*): Then you're not the one to break the
spell, that's for sure.

QUEEN: Honestly, I don't know what to think. On the one
hand, I have my heart set on you and Angela getting
married.

ANGELA: So have I!

QUEEN: But on the other hand, I certainly wouldn't want to
force you into anything.

KING: Well, I don't see what we can do except call the
whole thing off.

ANGELA (*Unhappily*): Call it off? Oh, no! We can't call it
off! It's what I want more than anything in the world!
I'll put up with anything, if only I can marry Frederick
—I mean, Croaker.

FRED (*Hopefully*): Anything, Angela? Even—even warts?

ANGELA (*Gulping*): Even—even warts. If they're little ones.

FRED (*Happily*): Oh, Angela, I—(*Suddenly he begins to
make croaking sounds.*) Murp! Murp!

QUEEN: Listen!

KING: It's working!

QUEEN: The spell is breaking!

KING: He's changing back!

FRED (*In a croaking voice*): You've done it, Angela! You've done it! I'm turning back into a frog! I'll never forget you for this, Angela. Never! (*He leapfrogs onto a stool, from there onto chest, and from there out window.*)

QUEEN (*Rushing to window*): Look! He's halfway back to the pond by now!

KING (*At window*): And he's halfway back to being a frog by now, too. Oh, Angela, I'm proud of you. You broke the spell!

ANGELA (*Sobbing*): But it's not fair, Daddy! I love him— and now he's gone! I'll never see him again.

QUEEN (*Going to her, soothingly*): There, there, darling. It's probably all for the best. (*Thoughtfully*) Of course, you know the old saying: Love conquers all.

ANGELA (*Hopefully*): You mean—?

QUEEN (*Wisely*): Stranger things have happened, Angela. Try thinking about him with all your might.

ANGELA (*Intensely, closing her eyes tight*): I love you, Croaker! I love you, Croaker! I—murp! Murp! (*She opens her eyes wide with delight, then quickly leaps from stool to chest.*)

QUEEN (*Enthusiastically*): She did it!

KING (*Shouting out window, happily*): Wait for Angela, Croaker! You're going to be married after all! (ANGELA *leaps out window.*)

QUEEN (*Wiping a tear from her eye*): Oh, Marmaduke. Isn't young love beautiful? It—it reminds me of when we were their age.

KING: Yes, but I still hate to see Angela go off like this. I'll—I'll miss her.

QUEEN (*Patting his hand*): Well, try to think of it this way, darling. It's not so much that we're losing a daughter. We're gaining a couple of frogs! (*Curtain*)

THE END

The Ten-Year-Old Detective

How to solve a baffling crime

Characters

PETER PIPER, *the ten-year-old detective*
JOHN, *his partner*
MARMADUKE, *a talkative gangster*
MORTIMER, *a quiet gangster*

SETTING: *The Peter Piper Detective Agency office, in Pete's house. A desk and chair are at center, and another chair is beside desk.*

AT RISE: PETE *is sitting in chair. He wears a fake moustache.* JOHN *is sitting at the desk. Both stare into space.*

PETE (*Suddenly jumping up*): Hark! Was that a knock at the door?

JOHN (*Bored*): There was no knock at the door.

PETE: Then it must have been the telephone ringing.

JOHN: The telephone didn't ring.

PETE: Then I must be hearing things. Business is so slow I'm losing my mind.

JOHN (*Dryly*): I'll find it for you. Hand me the magnifying glass.

PETE (*Disgruntled*): Very funny. (*Paces up and down*) To think that I, Peter Piper, the best detective in the whole world—and only ten years old to boot!—should have to sit here idly, day after day, with nobody demanding my services. You'd think they'd be breaking down the door with their problems for me to solve. But, no! I'm doomed never to be recognized for the great detective I truly am.

JOHN: Maybe there just aren't any crimes being committed.

PETE: Why, that's ridiculous. As a matter of fact, a crime was committed right in this very house, this very morning, by my very mother.

JOHN: Your mother? What did she do?

PETE: She forced me to take a nap. A nap! Me—a ten-year-old kid!

JOHN: So what was the crime?

PETE (*Slowly and precisely*): Kid napping, you fool. (*The phone rings.*) Hark! A knock at the door!

JOHN (*Answering phone*): Peter Piper Detective Agency, the only agency in town featuring a ten-year-old detective. John Johnson speaking. . . . That's good. . . . That's bad. . . . That's good. . . . That's bad. . . . That's good. . . . That's bad. (*He hangs up.*)

PETE: What was that all about?

JOHN: I was helping him sort strawberries, of course. (*Mimics himself quietly*) That's good. . . . That's bad.

PETE: That's ridiculous! (*Dramatically putting his hand on his forehead*) Oh, where, where, *where* is the case that will make me famous? Something that will tax my incredible brain—call on all my cunning—challenge my every nerve—and earn me a few bucks into the bargain?

JOHN: Relax. You've only been in business since nine o'clock this morning.

PETE: Right! And here it is half-past two. A has-been in five and a half hours—and me only ten years old.

JOHN: Something will turn up. Believe me.

PETE: You really have faith in me?

JOHN: I wouldn't have agreed to be your partner if I didn't have faith in you. Who but Peter Piper solved the Little Miss Muffet Case?

PETE (*Swaggering*): The spider did it. The evidence never lies.

JOHN: Who but Peter Piper solved the Pig-Stealing Caper?

PETE: Tom, Tom the Piper's Son did it. The evidence never lies.

JOHN: Who but Peter Piper solved the Little Boy Blue Disappearance Mystery?

PETE: He was under a haystack, fast asleep. The evidence never lies. Yes, I'm forced to admit it: I'm Mr. Terrific.

JOHN: Well, I wouldn't say *that* . . .

PETE (*Menacingly*): Are you my partner? Do you believe in me?

JOHN (*Backing down*): All right, all right, you're Mr. Terrific.

PETE: Thanks. Good of you to say so. (*The phone rings.*) Hark! A knock at the door! The evidence never lies.

JOHN: You *are* out of practice. (*Answering phone*) Peter Piper Detective Agency. . . . You don't say. . . . You don't say. . . . You don't say. (*He hangs up.*)

PETE: Who was it?

JOHN: He didn't say.

PETE: Foiled again! I shall go mad, I tell you, mad, mad, mad! Have you ever seen a ten-year-old go mad, mad, mad? It's not a pretty sight, let me tell you.

JOHN: Relax, Pete. Whoever it was on the phone just now said he was coming right over. This could be the case you've been waiting for—your big chance.

PETE: Are you sure you're not just saying that so I won't go mad, mad, mad?

JOHN: Would Watson kid Sherlock Holmes? (*There is a knock at door, and* MARMADUKE *and* MORTIMER, *two*

1940s-movie-gangster types, burst in. Both are wearing lobster bibs.)

MARMADUKE: Is this the Peter Piper Detective Agency?

JOHN: It is.

MARMADUKE: Which one of you is Peter Piper, the ten-year-old detective?

JOHN (*Pointing to* PETE): He is.

MARMADUKE: Hm-m. He looks a lot older than ten to me. How come he has a moustache?

JOHN: He's precocious. Besides, it sounds better to say he's ten years old. Then people aren't disappointed when he doesn't solve a case.

MARMADUKE: Well, why doesn't your friend say something?

JOHN: Why doesn't *your* friend say something?

MARMADUKE: He's too upset to speak. He's suffered a terrible tragedy. That's why we're here.

PETE (*To* MORTIMER, *enthusiastically*): What seems to be the trouble, sir?

MARMADUKE (*Menacingly*): I told you, he's too upset to speak. I do all the talking. Right, boss?

MORTIMER (*In a very low, gravelly voice*): Right.

PETE (*To* MARMADUKE): In that case, sir, why don't *you* tell me what the problem is?

MARMADUKE (*Looking at* PETE *carefully*): You don't look too bright to me. Right, boss?

MORTIMER: Right.

MARMADUKE: In fact, I'm not sure we ought to give you our business. Right, boss?

MORTIMER: Right.

PETE: But you can't walk out on me!

MARMADUKE: Why not?

PETE: Because the door is locked. (*Putting his hand to his head, dramatically*) I tell you, if I don't get this case I shall go mad, mad, mad!

MARMADUKE: We wouldn't want that to happen, would we, boss?

MORTIMER: Right.

MARMADUKE: I've seen a ten-year-old kid go mad, mad, mad. It's not a pretty sight.

PETE: Then it's all settled. Now, what's the problem?

MARMADUKE: Somebody has stolen—

PETE (*Breaking in eagerly*): A necklace. Right?

MARMADUKE: Wrong.

PETE: A billfold! Right?

MARMADUKE: Wrong.

PETE: A treasure map! Right?

MARMADUKE (*Patiently, to* MORTIMER): Boss, I think maybe we ought to go somewhere else. Right?

MORTIMER: Right.

PETE (*On his knees, pleading*): No, anything but that, I beg you! (*Jumps up*) Here, I'll prove to you what a good detective I am. You had lobster for lunch. Right?

MARMADUKE (*Amazed*): Hey, that's right.

PETE (*To* MORTIMER): And *you* had lobster for lunch. Right?

MORTIMER: Right.

MARMADUKE: Say, maybe I misjudged you. You're pretty good.

PETE (*Smugly*): They don't call me Mr. Terrific for nothing. The evidence never lies.

JOHN: Now, perhaps, if you gentlemen will state the nature of your problem. . . .

MARMADUKE: Well, it was like this. Somebody has stolen the boss's girlfriend.

JOHN (*Taken aback*): I beg your pardon?

MORTIMER: Right. (*Breaks into gravelly song*) "Somebody stole my gal, somebody stole my pal. . . ."

PETE: I just discovered something else.

MARMADUKE: What's that?

PETE (*To* MORTIMER): You never sang at the Metropolitan Opera. Right?

MORTIMER: Right.

MARMADUKE: You really *are* good at this detective stuff, even if you are only ten years old.

PETE (*Modestly*): Well, I *am* going on eleven.

JOHN: Now about this missing young lady. . . .

MARMADUKE: Oh, yeah. Well, we were just coming out of the seafood restaurant down the street when a taxi pulled up. The three of us started for it. Naturally, we let the young lady get in first. But as soon as she stepped inside, the driver reached back, slammed the door on us, and drove off.

JOHN: I see. The young lady was inside the cab, but you two gentlemen were left on the curb.

MARMADUKE: You got the picture.

PETE: How would I recognize the young lady if I were to see her again?

MARMADUKE: That's easy. She'll be wearing one Kelly green glove.

PETE: Because she's peculiar, I suppose.

MARMADUKE: Don't get wise. Because she dropped the other one. Right, boss?

MORTIMER: No, left. (*Pulls glove from his pocket and holds it up*)

PETE (*Whipping out magnifying glass, and pacing up and down, staring at floor*): I must begin investigating at once.

MARMADUKE (*Puzzled*): Wouldn't it be better to look around near the restaurant?

PETE: I can't. I'm only ten years old. I'm not allowed to cross the street. Here, let me take a look at that glove. (*Takes glove*)

MARMADUKE: What good is that going to do?

PETE (*With a light, superior laugh*): Ah, the mind of the non-professional! We detectives never overlook a single scrap of evidence, no matter how meager.

MARMADUKE: Are you suggesting there's something cheap about those gloves? The boss paid fifteen dollars for them! Right, boss?

MORTIMER: Right. (PETE *spreads the glove out on the desk and examines it with his magnifying glass.*)

PETE: Aha! Oho! Hee hee! Gentlemen, we are in luck!

JOHN: What is it?

PETE: There are fingerprints on the glove. That means all we have to do is find the person whose prints these are and we'll know who done it. I mean, did it.

MARMADUKE (*Disgustedly*): How on earth will we know that from the fingerprints on the glove? She was taken off by a taxi!

PETE (*With his superior laugh, sprinkling powder on the glove*): Ah, the mind of the non-professional. I tell you, the evidence never lies. There! I believe I can make out the prints now.

JOHN: Do you recognize them?

PETE: You forget, I have a memory like an I.B.M. computer. I can recognize at sight every fingerprint that ever was. Yes! Yes! These are the fingerprints of—

MARMADUKE (*Anxiously*): Of who? I mean, of whom?

PETE: Of Peter Piper, the Ten-Year-Old Detective! I have solved the crime. I did it myself!

JOHN: But that's ridiculous! How could you have done it? You never even left the house.

PETE: I admit that's a puzzle. But I *must* have done it. The evidence never lies. Besides, I can't think of anybody else to suspect, and you don't think I'm going to end my first case without pointing the finger at *somebody,* do you?

John, do your duty. Call the police and have me arrested. The sooner the better. You can't have someone like me running around loose, a menace to society.

JOHN: But this is preposterous! You can't be serious!

PETE (*Dramatically*): Ah, but I am! I must end this life of crime, whatever the cost. (*Nobly*) John, pick up that telephone and make that call.

JOHN (*Looking at him, then picking up phone and dialing*): Operator? Get me the Happy Dale Sanitarium.

PETE (*Disgusted*): No, no, John. You want the police. You call the police when you're dealing with an arch criminal. You call the Happy Dale Sanitarium when you're dealing with a nut—someone who's gone mad, mad, mad.

JOHN (*Grimly*): I know.

PETE (*Outraged*): You mean you think I'm some kind of nut? You think I'm mad, mad, mad?

JOHN, MORTIMER, *and* MARMADUKE (*In unison*): The evidence never lies. (*Blackout and quick curtain*)

THE END

The Bride of Gorse-Bracken Hall

A fishy tale

Characters

MRS. GARGLE, *housekeeper*
MR. ATKINSON, *good-hearted fisherman*
PETUNIA GOODSWEET, *a girl of 19*
SIR EDWARD CHICHESTER
THE VICAR

TIME: *Mid-afternoon on a bright June day in any year between, say, 1770 and 1890, depending on what's convenient for the costumier.*

SETTING: *The parlor of the Chichester ancestral home, Gorse-Bracken Hall. Entrances down left and right. In one wall, a window covered with heavy draw draperies.*

AT RISE: *The dimly-lighted room is empty. Then* MRS. GARGLE, *an evil-looking housekeeper carrying a lighted candle in a candlestick, enters from left. She looks about the room furtively, then turns back to the doorway.*

MRS. GARGLE: You can come in here, Mr. Atkinson. There's no one about. (ATKINSON *enters. He is carrying a large basket covered with a burlap sack.*)

ATKINSON: The parlor? Are you sure you want a basket of fresh fish in the parlor?

MRS. GARGLE: Do as you are bid, Mr. Atkinson, and mind your own business. (*Gives a wild, evil laugh*) Ha, ha, ha, ha, ha!

ATKINSON: What's so funny?

MRS. GARGLE (*Snapping*): Nothing, you fool! That's just the normal laugh of an evil housekeeper such as I. We evil housekeepers are always laughing wildly—but never when there's anything funny. Now put that basket down.

ATKINSON: Very well. (*Puts down basket*) Here is the bill. (*Takes bill from pocket and hands it to her.*)

MRS. GARGLE (*Reading it over*): Six pounds of haddock . . . a dozen crabs . . . four perch . . . three dozen whitings . . . a peck of clams . . . two sardines . . . and seven pounds of salmon.

ATKINSON (*Suspiciously*): There's something fishy going on here!

MRS. GARGLE: What—what do you mean?

ATKINSON: Sir Edward has never ordered clams before.

MRS. GARGLE: Oh, that's easily explained. We're expecting company today for the—(*Suddenly catches herself.*) Whoops! I almost let slip one of the deep, dark secrets of Gorse-Bracken Hall.

ATKINSON (*Quickly*): Would the secret you were about to let slip have anything to do with Sir Edward Chichester and Miss Petunia Goodsweet?

MRS. GARGLE (*Laughing wildly*): Ha, ha, ha, ha, ha! (*Sudden change of tone to one of intensity and suspicion*) What are you hinting at, Atkinson? Do you know something, or are you merely guessing?

ATKINSON: All I know is this. Sir Edward Chichester is a handsome, eligible bachelor—even if he is confined to a wheelchair. For the last three months, a beautiful, noble, kind-hearted, dumb girl named Petunia Goodsweet has been living here as governess. Ordinarily, those facts in themselves would give rise to no gossip.

MRS. GARGLE (*Stiffly*): How could they?

ATKINSON: But when the baker in the village suddenly mentions—as he did this morning—that he has received orders for a wedding cake to be sent to Gorse-Bracken Hall . . . *and* when the Vicar lets slip—as he did this morning—that he has been asked to appear at Gorse-Bracken Hall prepared to preach a wedding service . . . why, then, a body just naturally begins drawing conclusions.

MRS. GARGLE: And what conclusions *have* you drawn from all this?

ATKINSON (*Scratching his head*): That's just the trouble. I can't seem to draw *any*. Something's going on here, but I haven't the foggiest notion what it could be.

MRS. GARGLE: And it's just as well for you that you don't. Sir Edward doesn't take kindly to outsiders interfering in what goes on at Gorse-Bracken Hall. (PETUNIA GOODSWEET *enters, dressed in a wedding gown. She is one of those creatures who manage to be radiant without being bright.*)

PETUNIA: Ah, Mrs. Gargle! And Mr. Atkinson, our dear old fisherman from our dear old village here in dear old England! But why so dark? Why so dreary? Let us open the curtains, Mrs. Gargle. Today of all days the house should be flooded with sunshine!

MRS. GARGLE: But keeping the curtains closed makes the room so pleasantly Gothic.

ATKINSON: Gothic? I'd call it Visigothic! (PETUNIA *opens the curtains; the room is flooded with light. At the same moment, a foghorn is heard.*)

PETUNIA: How odd! The sun is shining boldly—and yet they are sounding the foghorns.

ATKINSON: There's lots of odd things about this place, if you'll allow me to say so, Miss Goodsweet.

MRS. GARGLE: Hold your tongue, Atkinson! Least said, soonest mended, you know.

CHICHESTER (*From offstage*): Mrs. Gargle! Come here. I want you.

MRS. GARGLE: Ah, the master calls. I suggest, Mr. Atkinson, that you leave this house at once, before you start any mischief. (*Turns to* PETUNIA; *suddenly intense*) And as for *you,* you ugly, hateful, wicked, scheming, spiteful creature—

CHICHESTER (*From offstage*): Mrs. Gargle! (*She glares at* PETUNIA *and exits.*)

PETUNIA (*Thoughtfully*): I suppose it's foolish of me, but something tells me that Mrs. Gargle doesn't like me.

ATKINSON (*Urgently*): Oh, Miss Goodsweet—dear Miss Goodsweet—may I give you a friendly word of advice? Leave Gorse-Bracken Hall! Leave it at once! Little do you dream what peril you may find yourself in at any moment if you stay!

PETUNIA: Leave Gorse-Bracken Hall? But—but where would I go?

ATKINSON: Where did you live before you came here?

PETUNIA: Ah! I came straight from the orphanage where I had spent my entire life. Indeed, if I hadn't seen Sir Edward's advertisement for a governess, I might be living in the orphanage still.

ATKINSON: But doesn't it seem strange that you should be a governess in a house that has no children?

PETUNIA: Not really. As a matter of fact, it's quite perfect. You see, I'm a terrible governess. Really, Mr. Atkinson, I am sure your fears for me are groundless.

ATKINSON: Tell me, Miss Goodsweet. Have you not noticed workmen on the grounds of Gorse-Bracken Hall?

PETUNIA: Yes, now that you mention it. But what evil could that portend for me? Just because each night at midnight two men with shovels start digging in the ground outside my window, I see no cause for alarm.

ATKINSON: But *what* are they digging, Miss Goodsweet?

PETUNIA: I—I don't know. I've thought of asking—but I do hate to pry! (*Foghorn sounds.*)

PETUNIA: How odd! There's that foghorn again!

ATKINSON (*Darkly*): There are *lots* of odd things going on around here, Miss Goodsweet, if you want my opinion.

PETUNIA (*Sweetly*): I fear me you are too suspicious, Mr. Atkinson. Be as I am! Open! Trusting! Naïve! Dumb! I assure you it makes life *much* simpler! (SIR EDWARD CHICHESTER *enters from left, in his wheelchair. He is a handsome man, impeccably dressed from the waist up. From the waist down, he is completely covered with a lap robe.*)

CHICHESTER: Ah, my dear Miss Petunia, Mrs. Gargle told me I would find you here.

PETUNIA: Yes, Sir Edward. I was passing the time with Mr. Atkinson, our dear old fisherman from our dear old village in—

CHICHESTER (*Finishing for her, dryly*): Our dear old England. Yes, yes, you've spoken of him before.

ATKINSON (*Humbly*): I was just leaving, Sir Edward.

CHICHESTER: Oh, no, no, you mustn't leave, Atkinson. As a matter of fact, I will have particular need of your services in a little while.

ATKINSON: As you wish, Your Lordship.

PETUNIA: And how have you been feeling today, dear Sir Edward?

CHICHESTER: Can you wonder how I am feeling today, dear Miss Petunia? Today of all days? Why, I am the happiest man alive!

PETUNIA (*Gaily*): Oh, you are just saying that, dear Sir Edward!

CHICHESTER (*Wheeling himself close to her*): Must you go on calling me Sir Edward? After the promise you have given me, it seems to me to be too cold, too distant, too formal. From this day forward, you must call me something more intimate than Sir Edward.

PETUNIA: Edward?

CHICHESTER: Sir.

PETUNIA (*In rapture*): Sir!

CHICHESTER: And I shall call you Petunia. (*In ecstasy*) Oh, Petunia, Petunia, Petunia!

PETUNIA: Oh, Sir, Sir, Sir!

CHICHESTER: And you will really have me for your husband?

ATKINSON (*Aside*): What's this? What's this?

CHICHESTER: In spite of the fact that I am confined to a wheelchair?

PETUNIA (*Happily*): Oh, most truly, Sir! For you must know that I have loved you with a strange, smoldering passion ever since the first day I came here to Gorse-Bracken Hall.

ATKINSON (*Boldly*): Am I to understand, Sir Edward, that you plan to marry Miss Goodsweet?

CHICHESTER (*Coldly*): You understand precisely, Atkinson.

ATKINSON (*Protesting*): But you cannot! You cannot!

CHICHESTER: You forget yourself, Atkinson. I am Lord of the Manor. I can do anything I blame well please.

ATKINSON: But surely even *you* are not so cold-blooded that you would marry the girl without telling her the secret of Gorse-Bracken Hall? (*Urgently, to* PETUNIA) Ask him the secret, Miss Goodsweet—and do not marry him until he has told it.

PETUNIA: Oh! I—I don't know what to do!

CHICHESTER (*To* PETUNIA): Is there something you want to ask me? You know I will tell you anything you ask me, Petunia.

PETUNIA: Well, it's true there are one or two things that puzzle me. On the other hand, I hate the idea of saying anything that would upset the wedding plans. You've no idea how hard it is for us orphan governesses to find husbands!

ATKINSON: Ask him about the foghorns, miss!

CHICHESTER (*Laughing*): Is that what's bothering you, Petunia? I can explain that easily enough. (*He pulls an empty soda bottle from the basket attached to his chair, and blows across the opening, producing a foghorn sound.*) I make that sound myself. It reminds me of my boyhood, spent on the wild and windy shores of Cornwall. Surely there's nothing wrong in that?

PETUNIA (*Triumphantly*): I knew there was an explanation! Oh, Sir, I am the happiest bride that ever was!

ATKINSON: But—but—

CHICHESTER (*Coldly*): That's enough, Atkinson. (MRS. GARGLE *and* THE VICAR *enter left.*)

MRS. GARGLE: Sir Edward, the Vicar has arrived. We can begin the ceremony at any time.

VICAR: Oh, Sir Edward, what joy! To think that there is to be a wedding in Gorse-Bracken Hall after all these years! (*To* PETUNIA) Allow me to wish you every happiness, my dear. (*Extends a hand to* ATKINSON) And allow me to congratulate the happy bridegroom as well!

PETUNIA (*Brightly*): Why, how funny! I am not marrying Mr. Atkinson!

VICAR (*Confused*): Not marrying Mr. Atkinson? Then who (*As the light breaks*)—surely you aren't—that is, you don't mean to suggest—I mean, you don't plan to marry Sir Edward?

PETUNIA: Yes, I do.

VICAR (*Staggered*): But it's—it's impossible! Oh, Sir Edward, I appeal to you. Surely you can't seriously expect me to perform the sacred marriage ceremony over you and Miss Goodsweet?

CHICHESTER (*Coldly*): And why not, sir?

VICAR (*Shocked*): Why, the girl's not of our class!

CHICHESTER: Oh, don't be an old fuddy-duddy! If I'm willing to marry her, why shouldn't you oblige?

VICAR (*Shrugging*): Well, if you put it that way. . . . Where did you wish the ceremony to be performed?

CHICHESTER: I thought the library would be best. Mrs. Gargle, here, and Atkinson will be our witnesses.

VICAR: Very well, then. Shall we proceed?

ATKINSON: Stop! This travesty cannot go on! I declare an impediment!

MRS. GARGLE: Be quiet, Atkinson!

ATKINSON: I won't be quiet! Someone must tell the girl the truth—and if none of you will do it, I must do it myself.

PETUNIA (*Weakly*): Oh, Mr. Atkinson, whatever do you mean?

ATKINSON: Miss Goodsweet, it pains me to see you so pale and heartsick—but you must know the truth. There is a secret connected with Sir Edward Chichester, and I am determined to uncover it! (*He goes to* CHICHESTER *and pulls the lap robe from around him, revealing that the lower half of* CHICHESTER's *body is a fish tail.*) Behold, Miss Goodsweet! There is the truth about your pretty Sir Edward Chichester!

CHICHESTER (*Through clenched teeth*): Curse you, Atkinson! You'll pay for this!

VICAR: My word! He's a—a merman!

MRS. GARGLE (*Triumphantly*): I knew the marriage wouldn't take place!

CHICHESTER (*Brokenly*): Well, Petunia? Do you say nothing? Surely you have some words for me? A cry of outrage? A shriek of disgust? A heartrending curse?

PETUNIA (*Matter-of-factly*): You mean just because you're part fish? Oh, Sir, that doesn't bother me in the least.

ATKINSON (*Staggered*): Not bother you?

PETUNIA: Why should it? Nobody's perfect.

CHICHESTER (*Happily*): And you will marry me anyway?

PETUNIA: Of course I will. Though I must say I'm curious to meet the rest of your family.

CHICHESTER: Mother will come and pay us a visit—just as soon as the workmen finish digging that swimming pool for her under your window!

MRS. GARGLE (*Resigned*): Well, it seems there's to be a new mistress at Gorse-Bracken Hall after all. I suppose we might as well get on with it. Shall we go into the library, then?

PETUNIA: By all means. Coming, Mr. Atkinson? (MRS. GARGLE, PETUNIA, *and* ATKINSON *exit right.*)

VICAR: Shall I push you, Sir Edward, or will you propel yourself?

CHICHESTER: Oh, I can manage. Er, tell me—I've never been married before, and the subject is rather embarrassing—but I *must* ask . . .

VICAR: Yes?

CHICHESTER: Do you send me a bill for your services, or am I supposed to send you a check?

VICAR (*Lightly*): Oh, mercy, why bother about anything so formal? After the ceremony, why don't you just slip me a fin? (*Quick curtain*)

THE END

The Last Time I Saw Paris

A visitor to Mount Olympus

Characters

ATHENE
HERA
       APHRODITE
       PARIS

SETTING: *Mount Olympus. Stone benches stand left and right.*

AT RISE: HERA *is seated on one bench, polishing a thunderbolt, of which there is a pile on the floor beside her.* ATHENE, *seated on other bench, pushes her helmet back, then stretches and yawns.*

ATHENE (*Impatiently*): Another boring day on Mount Olympus.

HERA: Now, now, Athene. Why don't you take up some hobby? You're so good at arts and crafts I don't see why you can't keep busy. (*She blows on thunderbolt, then rubs it hard with cloth, and holds it at a distance to inspect it.*)

ATHENE (*Shaking her head as she waves her hand in irritation*): Do you call polishing thunderbolts keeping busy? I call it busy work. Pretty dull, if you ask me.

HERA: Well, why don't you go inspect your olive grove?

ATHENE (*Bored*): You've seen one olive tree, you've seen them all.

HERA: Then how about reading a good book? After all, you *are* the goddess of wisdom.

ATHENE: Books bore me. (*Rises and begins to pace back and forth restlessly*) I want something new to happen —something exciting!

HERA: You could always see how your friend Jason is getting along with the *Argo*.

ATHENE: No, he's away on a shakedown cruise before going off after the Golden Fleece, and you know I always get seasick. Oh, there's simply nothing to do.

HERA: I feel sorry for you. I never have trouble keeping busy. Only the other day when I went down to Earth I got involved in an interesting case.

ATHENE (*Sarcastically*): I can just imagine!

HERA: No, really. It was a sad case, rather touching, in fact. There was this young musician, Orpheus, who had lost his wife, Eurydice. She was killed by a snake and ended up in Hades.

ATHENE (*Bored*): Oh? (*Yawns*)

HERA: His pleas really got to me, so I arranged for him to go down to Hades to try to get his wife back.

ATHENE: How did he make out?

HERA: Last I knew, he was down there playing his lyre and it looked as if he would charm them all and get her back.

ATHENE: Well, Hera, that may be all right for you, but that's not what I call exciting. I'd like some real adventure.

HERA (*Looking offstage*): Maybe it's on its way. Here comes Aphrodite with the mail. Maybe there's a letter for you from Odysseus.

ATHENE: I think he has his hands full with Penelope. (*Sighing*) I'm sure Aphrodite gets plenty of mail. She's goddess of love. Everyone writes to her with their problems.

She ought to set up a marriage counseling service to answer all those "Dear Aphie" letters. (*Sighs*) But me— all I ever get are catalogs from mail order houses selling do-it-yourself kits. (APHRODITE *enters, carrying some letters and a golden apple.*)

APHRODITE (*Waving letters as she approaches* HERA *and* ATHENE): Girls! Girls! The afternoon mail is here.

ATHENE: Anything for me?

APHRODITE: Just a bill from your helmet polisher. (*Hands her envelope, then turns to* HERA) And there's a bill for you from your sandal shop. Those gold sandals certainly must set you back a lot. (*Hands* HERA *envelope, then looks at postcard in her hand*) And there's also a postcard here.

HERA: For me? I wonder who—

APHRODITE (*To* ATHENE): It's one of those garish, touristy things. (*Reading*) "Greetings from the Underworld." (*Gives postcard to* HERA)

HERA (*Reading it*): Well, isn't this nice. "Having wonderful time, wish you were here. Signed, Orpheus."

ATHENE: Well, so much for the mail as a possible source of amusement!

APHRODITE: Wait! There was something else. Look! (*She holds up gold apple.*)

HERA: What is it, dear?

APHRODITE: It's a golden apple. It just came in the mail.

ATHENE: Well, who is it for?

APHRODITE: That's the curious part of it. I'm not sure. The label just says, "For the fairest of the fair."

ATHENE (*Suddenly sitting up straight*): The fairest of the fair?

APHRODITE: That's what the label says.

HERA (*Innocently*): Well, Aphrodite, dear, I think it *must* be meant for you. Don't you agree, Athene?

ATHENE (*Shrugging; overly casual*): Probably.

APHRODITE (*With exaggerated modesty*): Why, you girls must be joking! Surely you don't mean to suggest that I—why, it's too silly for words. I thought surely it must belong to one of *you* two.

HERA (*In mock amazement*): To me? Now, really, Aphrodite, how could anyone possibly think that I could be the fairest of the fair? I mean, dear, I'm older than you.

APHRODITE (*Deprecatingly*): Just because you're years older—

HERA (*Overly sweet*): Let's not get carried away, dear. I said I was older—I didn't say I was *years* older.

APHRODITE: Hera, you know what the Delphic Oracle says. "Age lies not heavily on those who lie lightly."

HERA (*Shaking her head, perplexed*): One of these days we must get a new translator for the Delphic Oracle.

ATHENE: But, Hera, if *you* refuse the apple, surely you don't think *I* . . . ?

APHRODITE (*Quickly*): But of course, Athene, darling, the apple is yours. Who else on Olympus has a figure like yours?

ATHENE: Well, but what about Hera's complexion?

HERA: And what about Aphrodite's hair?

APHRODITE: But really, Hera, when you consider Athene's lovely eyes—

ATHENE: And your perfect nose, Aphrodite! Let's not forget your perfect nose! And Hera's mouth. Hera, you must admit your mouth is—well, perfection.

HERA: My mouth! But, Athene, your ear lobes—

APHRODITE (*Interrupting*): Athene is right about your mouth, Hera—

ATHENE (*Interrupting*): And there's Aphrodite's posture to take into account—

HERA (*Interrupting*): Not to mention your graceful carriage—

APHRODITE (*Raising her hands for silence*): Girls, girls, girls! It's obvious none of us can agree as to who really gets the golden apple.

HERA: I suggest you just pitch the silly thing down from the top of Mount Olympus, dear. Maybe that way whoever really *is* the fairest of the fair will find it.

ATHENE: I was going to suggest just returning it to the Post Office marked "Return to Sender, Addressee Unknown."

APHRODITE: You're both right. That's just what I'll do. (*She starts out.*)

HERA (*Jumping up quickly, in alarm*): Er—Aphrodite!

ATHENE (*Simultaneously*): Wait a minute, Aphrodite!

APHRODITE (*Stopping, a knowing smile on her face*): Yes?

HERA (*Tactfully*): Dear . . . on second thought . . . not that it really matters, of course, but—well, wouldn't it be rude just to send the golden apple back?

ATHENE: Hera is right, Aphrodite. If someone was good enough to go to all the trouble of having an apple carved out of solid gold, the least we can do is find someone to accept it.

APHRODITE: I agree. But who?

ATHENE (*Staring off into space*): Well, just to solve the problem . . . as a favor to you girls . . . *I'd* be willing to—

HERA: No, Athene, I don't think you should. Since it would be so obvious to everyone that I couldn't *possibly* be the fairest of the fair, *I* should take it. I mean, that would be fair.

APHRODITE: Girls, I simply can't let you make such sacrifices. *I'm* the one who caused the problem by picking

the silly thing up in the first place. *I* should be the one
to *force* myself to keep the apple.

ATHENE (*Dryly*): I think we're right back where we started.

APHRODITE: Honestly, how anyone ever expected three
women to be able to agree on which one is the most
beautiful. . . .

HERA: That's it!

ATHENE: That's what?

HERA (*Profoundly*): The one below must go above to find
the one in three!

APHRODITE: *What?*

ATHENE: Don't mind her, she's quoting that darned
Delphic Oracle again.

HERA: What we need is a man—a human being—an earth-
ling.

APHRODITE: Why, that's a marvelous idea, Hera!

HERA (*Closing her eyes, intoning*): Let the first human
man to pass beneath this spot be brought before us instantly! I, Hera, command it!

ATHENE (*Jumping up and down*): Oh, this is so exciting!
I wonder who it'll be?

APHRODITE: Oh, I hope he's handsome!

ATHENE: I hope he's intelligent!

HERA (*Dryly*): I hope he appreciates older women. (PARIS
*enters. He is a young man, considerably less mature
than the goddesses.*)

ATHENE: Behold! He comes!

APHRODITE: Good morrow, stranger!

HERA: Welcome to our dwelling place!

PARIS: Oh, hi, there! Say, do you know what place this is?
I think I'm lost.

HERA: What is your name, earth person?

PARIS: My name? I'm Paris, Prince of Troy. Pleased to

meet you. I seem to have lost my sense of direction. This isn't one of the suburbs of Troy, is it?

HERA (*Imperiously*): It is for us to question. It is for you to be silent and obey.

PARIS: Huh? Boy, that's all Greek to me.

HERA: Let your eyes do my bidding and let your choice be my choice.

PARIS: Gee, lady, did anyone ever tell you you sound just like the Delphic Oracle? I'm getting out of here! (*He starts to exit.* APHRODITE, *smiling sweetly, stops him.*)

APHRODITE: Just a moment, kind sir. Please. You will do us a great favor if you stay.

PARIS: Well . . . anything to oblige a pretty girl, I always say.

ATHENE (*Thrusting apple at him*): Do you see this apple?

PARIS (*Taking it happily*): Gee, thanks! I haven't had lunch yet, and I love apples!

APHRODITE: No, no. You don't understand. That's not a real apple. It's solid gold.

PARIS: Solid gold! Wow! I'll bet it must have cost a lot of money—more than my season's ticket to the Olympic Games, even. Gee, *thanks,* girls! I sure appreciate this!

HERA (*Angrily*): No, no, no! The apple is not for you.

PARIS (*Disappointed*): Aw, shucks. I was afraid of that.

ATHENE: What we want you to do is hand that golden apple to whichever one of us you think is the fairest of the fair.

PARIS: The fairest of the fair, huh? Well, gee, you're *all* good-looking girls. I don't see how I could possibly decide which one of you is the prettiest.

HERA (*Patiently*): We understand your problem. All three of us, we admit, are more beautiful than any woman you have ever seen before. But one of us must be just a teeny, tiny bit prettier than the other two. And that's the one we want you to give the apple to.

PARIS (*Shaking his head*): Gee, I just don't see how I could—

APHRODITE: Paris, could I have a private word with you for a moment? (*She draws him to one side.*) Obviously, Paris, this whole thing is just a sort of game with us. I mean, none of us really takes it seriously. And since it obviously doesn't make any difference to you which one of us gets the apple, here's what I'll do. If you give me the apple, I'll get you a date with the most beautiful girl in the world: Helen, Queen of Sparta.

PARIS (*Impressed*): Wow! You really could? You have her phone number and everything?

APHRODITE: Trust me, Paris. I've got connections.

HERA (*Calling*): Paris! May I have a word with you in private?

PARIS (*Crossing to* HERA): Of course.

HERA (*Smoothly*): Now, Paris, you understand that the choice is to be all your own. But since you seem to be having such difficulty, I thought I could help you out. Choose me, Paris, and you know what I'll do?

PARIS: What?

HERA: I'll make you the richest man in the world.

PARIS (*Impressed*): Gee! You mean richer than King Croesus? (HERA *nods.*)

ATHENE (*Calling and beckoning with her finger*): Paris . . .

PARIS (*Crossing to* ATHENE): You want to make things easier for me, too, I'll bet.

ATHENE: Give the apple to me, and I promise you that for the rest of your life you will always be victorious in battle.

PARIS (*Impressed*): Really? Would that mean I could beat up Achilles? He's always showing off his muscles.

ATHENE (*Nodding*): When you get through with him, Achilles will look like a Greek ruin.

APHRODITE (*Calling*): Paris! Are you ready? We're waiting for your decision. (*Goddesses line up, facing him.*)

ATHENE: Paris—remember Athene!

HERA: Paris—remember Hera!

APHRODITE: Paris—remember Queen Helen of Sparta! ATreus 7-5609!

PARIS: Oh, wow! (*Tosses the apple to* APHRODITE, *who catches it.*) Aphrodite, the golden apple is yours!

APHRODITE (*Running off with it, joyfully*): Thanks, Paris! Thanks! (*Exits*)

HERA (*Seething*): Yes, Paris. Thanks. Thanks for nothing!

PARIS (*Concerned*): Oh, gee. You two aren't sore, are you? I mean, I had to pick one of you—so naturally two of you got left out. But I hope there aren't any hard feelings.

ATHENE (*Overly sweet*): Hard feelings? Why, no! Not at all!

HERA (*With venom*): Why should we care if you picked Aphrodite? Fair is fair.

ATHENE: As a matter of fact, I think we ought to give Paris a present, Hera—something to show him we have no hard feelings.

HERA: Good idea, Athene! Paris, we're going to give you a wonderful present, too, just the way Aphrodite did.

PARIS (*Happily*): You are? Gee! What is it going to be?

ATHENE *and* HERA (*Shouting at him in unison*): A Trojan horse! (*Quick curtain.*)

THE END

Hen Party

A dangerous dinner date

Characters

HENNY PENNY
GOOSEY POOSEY
DUCKY LUCKY

TURKEY LURKEY
CHICKEN LICKEN

SETTING: *Living room of Henny Penny's house. A sofa is at left center. In front of it is a tea table set for tea, with cups, saucers, spoons, napkins and teapot. Up center, an arched doorway leads to hall and front door. At right is a door leading to the rest of the house. Several comfortable chairs are set about the room.*

AT RISE: HENNY PENNY *is arranging the tea table, when* GOOSEY POOSEY *enters.*

HENNY: Ah, Goosey Poosey! How nice to see you again, my dear.

GOOSEY (*Looking about*): Aren't the other girls here yet?

HENNY: No, you're the first one.

GOOSEY: Who else have you invited?

HENNY: Oh, the usual crowd. Turkey Lurkey, Ducky Lucky . . .

GOOSEY: You didn't invite Chicken Licken, did you?

HENNY (*A bit taken aback*): Why, yes, as a matter of fact, I did.

GOOSEY (*Disappointed*): Oh, dear.

HENNY: What's the matter? I thought you liked Chicken Licken.

GOOSEY (*Hastily*): Oh, I do, I do. She's my dearest friend. It's just that—well, I suppose I can speak frankly to you, Henny Penny.

HENNY: You know that your secrets never pass my beak, Goosey Poosey.

GOOSEY: Well, the fact is there's a new bachelor in town. And my dear, he's divine!

HENNY (*With a sigh*): Ah, so *that's* the problem. A new bachelor. You think that once he sees Chicken Licken, the rest of us won't stand a chance. Just because she's a couple of years younger than we are—

GOOSEY (*Interrupting*): Let's face it, my dear. You and I aren't spring chickens.

HENNY (*Angrily*): It's not as if I were an old hen!

GOOSEY: But you know what men are like, Henny Penny.

HENNY (*Glumly*): I wish I did! (DUCKY LUCKY *enters*.)

DUCKY (*Bursting with gossip*): Girls! Wait till you hear the news!

HENNY: You mean about the new bachelor in town?

DUCKY (*Crestfallen*): Oh, then you already know. I wonder if Turkey Lurkey has heard.

GOOSEY (*Pointedly*): *I* wonder if Chicken Licken has heard.

HENNY: Honestly, it makes me so mad that the rest of us don't stand a chance once the boys get a look at Chicken Licken.

DUCKY: Are you telling me? Before she moved into the barnyard, Drakey Lakey and I were practically going steady. Then he got a look at *her*—and flew the coop!

GOOSEY: Drakey Lakey isn't the only fowl in the barnyard.

DUCKY (*Morosely*): He's the only one I want.

HENNY: But my dear, one thing we must all learn is not to put all our eggs into one basket.

GOOSEY (*Snidely*): Look who's clucking! What about you and Cocky Locky?

HENNY (*Unhappily*): All right, you don't have to rub it in. I'm as bad as Ducky Lucky.

DUCKY: Ducky Un-lucky is more like it.

GOOSEY: The question is, what are we going to do?

HENNY: What *can* we do? Chicken Licken is younger than we are, and she's prettier.

DUCKY: Well, I, for one, don't believe she's a natural blonde.

GOOSEY (*Gasping*): You mean—

DUCKY: Her feathers may be yellow, but have you noticed how dark her quills are?

GOOSEY (*In confidential tone*): You know I never say anything about anyone unless I can say something good. (*Dryly*) And is this good!

HENNY (*Avidly*): What?

DUCKY: Tell, tell!

GOOSEY: I heard that the time Chicken Licken said she was going off to visit her cousin, the Little Red Hen, she *really* went to have her beak straightened.

DUCKY: Why, that's positively fowl!

GOOSEY: I had it from a very good source. The Ugly Duckling! And look what cosmetic surgery did for *him*! (TURKEY LURKEY *enters up center.*)

HENNY: Here's Turkey Lurkey.

GOOSEY: Oh, hello. (*Admiringly*) I just *love* your new feathers, Turkey Lurkey.

TURKEY (*Pretending indifference*): What, these old things?

You've seen them a hundred times. I've had them ever since I moulted.

DUCKY: Well, you look splendid. I believe you've even lost some weight. Been dieting?

TURKEY (*With a sigh*): Yes, I always go on a diet this time of year, what with Thanksgiving coming.

GOOSEY: Don't remind me!

HENNY: Well, dear, don't look to me for sympathy. With me, weight control is a year-round thing. You know what the farmer believes in—chicken every Sunday!

TURKEY: Speaking of chicken . . . where's Chicken Licken?

DUCKY: She'll be along presently, no doubt.

TURKEY: I assume you all know about the new bachelor in town. (*They all nod.*) I wouldn't put it past Chicken Licken to be out on a date with him this very minute!

GOOSEY: But he just arrived, my dear. How could she get to know him so fast?

TURKEY: Who do you think is president of the Welcome Wagon?

DUCKY (*Gasping*): Oh, girls, she's right!

GOOSEY (*Angrily*): I for one have had it. The rest of you can take a defeatist attitude if you want, but I'm not going to let Chicken Licken go on stealing hearts as if she were the only bird on the block. I think it's time we began to fight back.

TURKEY: Fight back?

DUCKY: But how?

GOOSEY: If only we could get to meet this bachelor, I'm sure one of us girls could manage to interest him.

HENNY: Meet him? I don't even know his name.

DUCKY: His name is Foxy Loxy—and talk about gorgeous!

GOOSEY: Tall, broad-shouldered, teeth so white he could

be making TV toothpaste commercials, and the most beautiful red hair you've ever seen. If I could just meet him, I'm sure I would appeal to his taste!

HENNY (*Naïvely*): Why don't you just ask Chicken Licken to introduce you?

DUCKY: Oh, Henny Penny, you are so innocent.

GOOSEY: Chicken Licken would never introduce one of us to any eligible male. Oh, she'd *say* she would do it, but then she'd find some excuse to keep putting it off. Believe me, Henny Penny, I know Chicken Licken better than anyone. She's my dearest friend. I tell you she's a sneaking, conniving, scheming, devious (CHICKEN LICKEN *enters.* GOOSEY POOSEY *sees her, and without a break goes on speaking.*)—darling, lovely girl.

CHICKEN: Who is this you're raving about, Goosey Poosey?

GOOSEY (*In mock surprise*): Why, Chicken Licken! I didn't know you'd arrived. As a matter of fact, I was just talking about you, and wondering what was keeping you.

CHICKEN: Oh, I had a little accident on the way over. Sorry to be late, Henny Penny.

TURKEY: Not a serious accident, I hope.

CHICKEN: No, not really. I was driving my convertible with the top down when something hit me on the head. It was an acorn, I think.

HENNY: Oh, how unpleasant!

CHICKEN (*Rubbing her head*): It hurts a little—but I'm sure it's nothing.

GOOSEY (*Settling down to gossip*): Well, Chicken Licken. (*Pointedly*) Anything new?

CHICKEN: New? I don't think so . . . Oh, there is *one* thing. (*Others exchange knowing looks.*) Do you know that cave down the road? It's been rented to an absolutely horrid creature called Foxy Loxy. Honestly, I don't know why we couldn't have got some interesting neighbors for a change.

GOOSEY (*Not believing a word*): You say Foxy Loxy is horrid?

CHICKEN: The worst! I *had* to call on him—you know my position with the Welcome Wagon. But believe me, I was glad to get away as soon as I decently could.

HENNY: Why? What's wrong with this Foxy Loxy? He's not unattractive, is he?

CHICKEN: Oh, he's nice enough looking, I suppose, if you like the type. But his manners! He just kept *devouring* me with his eyes. He actually had the nerve to say that he thought I was so pretty, I made his mouth water. Isn't that disgusting?

DUCKY (*With a sigh*): If only some eligible bachelor would say that to me!

CHICKEN: Believe me, Ducky Lucky, this one is definitely to be avoided. I have to go back there when I leave here, and how I dread it.

GOOSEY: You say you can't stand the man, but you're going back to see him again?

CHICKEN: Yes, I forgot to give him the Welcome Wagon basket of goodies.

TURKEY (*With mock sympathy*): Poor Chicken Licken! What a dreadful thing to look forward to—a visit with a handsome, redheaded bachelor. My heart bleeds for you.

CHICKEN: If only there were some way I could get out of it!

GOOSEY (*Suddenly getting a brainstorm; overly sweet*): Chicken, darling, let me take a look at that bump on your head for a minute.

CHICKEN: Oh, it's nothing.

GOOSEY (*Insistently*): You can't be too careful, Chicken Licken. (*Inspects the back of* CHICKEN'*s head; in alarmed tone*) Oh! Oh, my dear!

CHICKEN (*Nervously*): What is it?

GOOSEY (*Exaggeratedly*): My dear! This is no ordinary acorn bump.

CHICKEN (*Frightened*): It—it isn't?

GOOSEY: Why, no! It looks to me more as though you were hit on the head by—by some bolt from the blue. Yes, that's it! A piece of sky fell and hit you!

CHICKEN: A piece of sky? I never heard of such a thing.

GOOSEY (*Quickly*): It doesn't happen very often. But when it does, it can be very, very serious. I think you ought to go into the kitchen this minute and wash the wound out with warm water.

CHICKEN: But, really—it feels like nothing at all.

GOOSEY: That's the way it always is with sky bumps. You just listen to me, dear. You go right in there (*Pointing to door right*) and wash it out this minute!

CHICKEN (*Tentatively*): All right, Goosey Poosey. If you say so . . . (*She goes out, right.*)

HENNY (*Calling after her*): Be sure to wash it out thoroughly, dear.

TURKEY: Is the wound really that serious, Goosey Poosey?

GOOSEY: Don't be a simpleton, Turkey Lurkey. I just needed an excuse to get Chicken Licken out of the room. Listen! I have a plan for meeting Foxy Loxy.

DUCKY: But Chicken Licken said he was horrid.

GOOSEY: My dear Ducky Lucky, sometimes you are too simple for words. The only reason Chicken Licken said what she did was to keep us from meeting him!

HENNY: But what can we do?

GOOSEY: Here's my plan. When Chicken Licken comes back in here, we must all tell her how ill she looks. We

have to convince her that the blow on her head is serious, and that she must lie down immediately. Then,
we'll offer to take the Welcome Wagon basket to Foxy
Loxy!

DUCKY: Do you think she'll fall for it?

GOOSEY: We'll *make* her fall for it. (*Looking off*) Quiet!
Here she comes. (CHICKEN LICKEN *re-enters*.) Well, dear,
did you wash the place where the sky fell on you?

CHICKEN: Yes, but I still don't feel anything.

GOOSEY (*Triumphantly*): That proves it's serious! You're
numb! You must lie down at once.

CHICKEN: Lie down? But I feel fine.

GOOSEY: You don't look fine. Does she, Ducky Lucky?

DUCKY (*Puzzled*): What? (*Suddenly*) Oh, no, Chicken
Licken, you really don't look well at all.

HENNY (*Helping* CHICKEN LICKEN *to lie down on sofa*):
You really must lie down at once, Chicken Licken.

TURKEY: Yes, lie perfectly still for at least an hour.

CHICKEN: But—but I can't lie here for an hour. I have to
take the Welcome Wagon basket to Foxy Loxy.

GOOSEY (*Grandly*): *We'll* take the basket to Foxy Loxy.
After all, what are friends for?

CHICKEN (*Sitting up*): Oh no, I really can't let you do that.
Foxy Loxy is evil, Goosey Poosey. You don't know what
he's like! He has teeth like knives—and his claws are like
daggers!

GOOSEY: Now, Chicken Licken, you're not to worry about
us. After all, there's safety in numbers. What harm can
this Foxy Loxy possibly do to us?

CHICKEN (*Relenting*): Well, if you're sure you don't
mind. . . .

GOOSEY: Not in the least.

DUCKY: Our dearest wish is to help you out, Chicken
Licken.

TURKEY: So even if going to see this Foxy Loxy is unpleasant and distasteful—

HENNY: We're prepared to make the sacrifice, for *your* sake.

CHICKEN (*Sinking back*): Oh, you girls are all so good to me! How can I ever repay you?

GOOSEY: Don't even think of it, my dear. Virtue is its own reward.

CHICKEN: You'll find the Welcome Wagon basket in the back seat of my car.

GOOSEY: Excellent. Coming, girls? (*She heads for the door, center, followed by* HENNY PENNY, DUCKY LUCKY, *and* TURKEY LURKEY.)

DUCKY (*Gaily; singsong*): We're going to meet Foxy Loxy! We're going to meet Foxy Loxy! (*Dryly*) Drakey Lakey, eat your heart out! (*The four go out.*)

CHICKEN: Oh, what good friends I have! If only they weren't going to see Foxy Loxy. I just know that creature is up to no good! (*Sighs*) Well, who knows? Maybe they'll all like each other. Wouldn't that be nice? They could all have a pleasant visit together. Maybe Foxy Loxy would even end up serving them a meal. Wouldn't that be splendid—if Foxy Loxy had them all for dinner! Oh, *wouldn't* that be a happy ending! (*She smiles blissfully. Quick curtain*)

THE END

Sail On! Sail On!

Columbus makes headlines

Characters

NICCOLO, *first mate*
LUIS, *second mate*
CHRISTOPHER COLUMBUS
HARRY ⎤
KATE ⎬ *newspaper reporters*
FRANK ⎦

SETTING: *A room in Columbus's apartment in Spain. A plain wooden table, small cabinet and several broken-down chairs furnish the room.*

AT RISE: *NICCOLO, a young sailor, stands at the door, right, looking off. LUIS, another sailor, lounges in a chair.*

LUIS: Any sign of him yet?

NICCOLO (*Turning toward room*): Not yet.

LUIS: But he must come soon! Time is running out.

NICCOLO: Isn't tomorrow as good as today?

LUIS: Nope. Today's the last day of the big boat sale. Three for the price of two. The sale ends tonight at nine o'clock. If Columbus doesn't have the money by then, it's goodbye exploration—and goodbye Columbus!

117

NICCOLO (*Doubtfully*): I don't think the Queen will give him the money.

LUIS: Never underestimate Columbus when he starts talking!

NICCOLO: But how is he ever going to persuade the Queen that the world is round—when everyone knows it's flat?

LUIS: He'll probably use the standing-an-egg-on-its-end routine.

NICCOLO: That old gag? That wouldn't convince a baby.

LUIS: Don't be too sure. I hear that Isabella's no scientific genius.

NICCOLO: Well, even if she doesn't give him the cash to buy the ships, maybe she'll give him enough to buy us some decent food. (LUIS *rises, goes over to cabinet*.)

LUIS (*Opening door of cabinet*): What do we have left in the larder?

NICCOLO: Just what's left of that food package Columbus's mother sent last month from Italy. A couple of moldy peanut butter and mozzarella sandwiches, and some dried-up Genoa salami. (*Sound of loud footsteps and whistling are heard.*)

LUIS: Listen! I think I hear Columbus coming now! (CHRISTOPHER COLUMBUS *enters from right, carrying a small paper sack. He strikes pose in doorway. He is a very dramatic fellow, and does everything with a flourish.*)

COLUMBUS (*Declaiming*): Sail on! Sail on! Sail on and on!

NICCOLO (*Greeting him happily*): Hey there, Columbus! How did it go?

LUIS (*Eagerly*): If that smile of yours means what I think it means, Queen Isabella gave you the dough!

COLUMBUS (*Grandly, moving into room and closing door behind him*): Not money, my boys—

NICCOLO and LUIS (*Disappointed*): Aw-w . . .

COLUMBUS: But something better than money! (*Waves*

paper sack) Look! She has given me a sack of jewels that I can use to buy my sailing vessels!

NICCOLO: Hey, let's see!

COLUMBUS (*Pouring contents of sack onto table*): Look at those gems! Diamonds, rubies, emeralds, sapphires! And, if my eyes mistake me not, she even threw in a few rhinestones and sequins for good measure.

LUIS: Why would the Queen be willing to sacrifice her jewels like that? Wouldn't it have been simpler just to write you a check?

COLUMBUS: The Queen is no fool, my boy. She only gave me what she didn't have any further use for. That necklace, for instance (*Pointing*)—they haven't been wearing things like that since 1489. Do you think the Queen would be caught wearing something that far out of date? Not if she intends to stay on the list of the Ten Best Dressed Queens of the Year!

NICCOLO (*Holding up earring*): Well, what's wrong with this earring? It looks O.K. to me.

COLUMBUS: She lost the other one. What good is one earring? The Queen may see herself as a style-setter, but wearing a single earring is too much even for her. Lucky for us, she has a habit of losing earrings.

LUIS (*Holding up silver bracelet*): Hey, what's this? (CO-LUMBUS *seizes it quickly and looks about in conspiratorial manner.*)

COLUMBUS: Hide that! If the King finds out about that, we'll all end up in the Spanish equivalent of the pokey.

LUIS: Why?

COLUMBUS: It's an I.D. bracelet the Queen got from a guy she went with before she met Ferdinand. You'll also find his high school ring in there.

NICCOLO (*Picking up ring*): Oh, here it is. Granada Boys' Technical School, Class of 1477.

COLUMBUS (*Grandly*): My lads, we're going to get the neatest set of matched sailing vessels that secondhand junk jewelry can buy. And then . . .

LUIS: And then?

COLUMBUS (*Grandly*): Sail on! Sail on! Sail on and on! (*Changes tone*) How late are the boat stores open?

NICCOLO: Till nine.

COLUMBUS: Good! I want to be sure there's enough time. I've called a little press conference. Niccolo, why don't you put out some refreshments? It's always good public relations to serve a little something to the press.

NICCOLO: I don't think they'll be too impressed by peanut butter and mozzarella.

COLUMBUS (*Grandly*): Then phone down for a pepperoni pizza.

NICCOLO (*Happily*): That's more like it! A little one or a big one?

COLUMBUS (*Handing him a piece of jewelry*): As big as you can get for a ruby-studded election button that says "Vote for Ferdinand for King."

NICCOLO (*Going off left*): One pepperoni pizza, coming right up! (*Exits*)

LUIS: Gosh, Columbus, it sure is exciting to think we're finally going to get our ships.

COLUMBUS (*Striking pose*): I can see them now!—the *Constitution*, the *Monitor*, and the *Merrimac*!

LUIS (*Doubtfully*): Aren't those names kind of corny?

COLUMBUS: Maybe you're right. Well, I'll come up with something. (*Knock at door is heard.*) Ah, that must be the reporters now. (*Rushes to mirror*) How do I look?

NICCOLO (*Entering from left*): I'll get the door.

LUIS (*Going to door, right*): I've already got it. (*Opens door. HARRY, KATE and FRANK, three reporters, enter.*

They are carrying steno pads; FRANK *also has a large sketch pad.*) Ah, the press! Come in, come in.

HARRY (*Hardboiled type*): Which one of you guys is the one with the hare-brained idea—(*Checks name scribbled on his pad*) Captain Christopher Columbus?

COLUMBUS: I am. And this is my first mate, Niccolo Piccolo, and my second mate, Luis Ruiz.

HARRY: Glad to meet you. I'm Harry Niña, from the Toledo *Sun-Times*. This is Kate Pinta, Lisbon *Daily News*, and that's Frank Santa Maria, *U.P.I.*

COLUMBUS (*Impressed*): United Press International?

FRANK: Upper Portugal *Independent*.

COLUMBUS: Mind if I make a note of your names? I always like to write my mother when I'm interviewed. Let's see. (*Takes pen from pocket, jots names on cuff*) Niña, Pinta, and Santa Maria. Say, those are catchy names!

KATE: Thanks. Now, can we get on with the interview, Chris?

COLUMBUS: Shoot!

HARRY: They say you're going to try to circ—circumna—circumnavi—to sail all the way around the world. What are you going to do when you get to the edge?

COLUMBUS (*Melodramatically*): Sail on! Sail on! Sail on and on!

FRANK (*Horrified*): But you'll fall off!

COLUMBUS: Never! The world is not flat—like a slice of bread. It's round—like a pizza!

KATE (*Sarcastically*): And I suppose the crust at the edge will keep you from falling off.

LUIS: Show them the standing-an-egg-on-its-end routine, Columbus.

HARRY: Skip it. I caught your act at the Palace.

FRANK: What's the point of this trip, Columbus?

COLUMBUS: I intend to reach the west by sailing east! I mean, reach the east by sailing west. One or the other, depending on how the wind blows. And I intend to return to Spain with a cargo of rice, silk, tropical fruits, spices, and some Japanese transistor radios. (*As reporters take notes*) Mark my words: This voyage is going to put Spain on the map! As a matter of fact, I've already hired a mapmaker named Amerigo Vespucci for that very purpose.

KATE: Is it true that Queen Isabella herself put up the money for this crazy journey?

COLUMBUS: She had no choice. I threatened to stick around the court doing my standing-an-egg-on-its-end routine every twenty minutes, until she gave in. (*Reporters take notes.*)

HARRY: And you're taking three ships on this journey?

COLUMBUS: That's right—the *Bach,* the *Beethoven,* and the *Brahms.*

FRANK: Where'd you ever get names like those? Nobody could ever remember them!

COLUMBUS: I just made them up. But maybe you're right. I'll keep working on it.

KATE: Well, I guess those are all the questions I have.

COLUMBUS: Good. It's getting late, and we've got to get down to the boat store before nine.

HARRY: What's the big rush?

NICCOLO: There's a sale on.

COLUMBUS: And on! Sail on and on!

KATE: Do you mind just posing for a few pictures, Chris, before we go?

COLUMBUS (*Happily*): Did you guys bring a camera with a flash attachment?

KATE: Don't be silly. They haven't been invented yet. No,

Frank, here, is a quick-sketch artist. (FRANK *opens sketch pad.*)

FRANK: Just hold still a minute. (*Drawing quickly, as* COLUMBUS *poses*) Got it! (*Turns over a page on his sketch pad.*) Now a profile shot. (COLUMBUS *turns his head profile.* FRANK *makes a few wild marks on pad, turns over page.*) Just one more. (*Repeats business*) O.K., let's go. I want to get these over to the darkroom in time for tonight's late edition.

COLUMBUS (*Hopefully*): Do you think I'll make the front page?

KATE (*Doubtfully*): Well, I don't know about that, Chris. There's not too much interest in travel articles right now, but we'll do the best we can.

HARRY (*As he and other reporters go out*): Well, take care now. See you in the funny papers. Ha, ha, ha! (*Closes door behind himself.*)

LUIS (*Outraged*): Did you hear that? The funny papers! The nerve of those reporters!

NICCOLO: Never mind, Columbus. They're just jealous that you're a man of vision and imagination.

COLUMBUS: Bah! That sort of thing doesn't bother me. *Any* kind of press coverage is good at this stage in my career. Besides, at least he didn't say they were going to run me in "Believe It or Not"!

NICCOLO: Let's forget them and go out to buy our ships.

COLUMBUS: Just let me gather up these jewels and I'll be with you. (*As he gathers jewels*) It burns me up to see how skeptical some people can be. I wish I could think of a way I could really hit the headlines. (*Paces back and forth*)

LUIS: Forget it, Columbus. Nobody's interested in explorers these days. You have to be a rock star before the newspapers treat you right. (COLUMBUS *stops suddenly.*)

COLUMBUS (*Triumphantly*): Hey! I've got it! Why didn't I think of this before?

NICCOLO (*Excitedly*): What is it, Columbus?

LUIS: Tell us!

COLUMBUS: We're not going to sail to the Indies after all!

LUIS *and* NICCOLO: We're not?

COLUMBUS: No! We're going to discover America!

NICCOLO (*Admiringly*): Oh, wow!

LUIS: That's a fantastic idea!

COLUMBUS (*Strutting*): *Then* we'll see about the headlines. The whole world will be talking about Christopher Columbus long after they've forgotten there ever was a (*Reads from cuff*)—*Niña,* a *Pinta,* and a *Santa Maria.* (*Changes tone, scratches his head*) There's something about those names that's very catchy.

LUIS: Hey, Niccolo! What ever happened to that pizza you ordered?

NICCOLO: Oh, I meant to tell you. The pizza shops are all closed.

COLUMBUS: They are?

NICCOLO: Yeah, I forgot. It's Columbus Day.

COLUMBUS (*Shrugging*): Well, you can't win 'em all. (*Points dramatically to door*) Sail on! Sail on! Sail on and on! (*They start out, laughing happily. Fast curtain*)

THE END

Happy Haunting!

A school for spooks

Characters

MISS MAGICIA, *headmistress*
MISS GOBLINETTE, *her secretary*
MRS. SPECTRE
WILMA WITCH
FANNY PHANTOM
POLLY POLTERGEIST

SETTING: *Office of Miss Magicia, in the Seminary for Young Spooks. A large desk, with a chair behind it and one at its side, are left center. At right, there are four straight chairs arranged in a semi-circle. On the desk is a telephone. There is a door at right.*
AT RISE: MISS MAGICIA *is seated at her desk. The phone rings and she answers it.*

MISS MAGICIA (*Into phone*): Miss Magicia's Seminary for Young Spooks. . . . Yes, this is Patricia Magicia speaking. . . . No, I'm sorry, but I absolutely cannot give interviews to the newspapers. . . . (*Indignantly*) No, I do *not* care to comment on the rumor that my school is going to merge with the Massachusetts Institute of Demonology. (*Sharply*) Young man, I don't care if every ghost academy in the country goes coeducational. Miss Magicia's Seminary for Young Spooks has always been an all-female institution, and it will remain an all-female institution as long as there's a lack of breath in my body! . . . I don't care what the leaders of the women's lib movement would have to say. They're nothing but a pack of—of witches! (*Slams down receiver.* MISS GOBLIN-ETTE, *her secretary, enters, carrying typed letters.*) Honestly, Miss Goblinette, these newspapers seem to think that the Headmistress of a school has nothing better to do than answer a lot of foolish questions. This is the worst day they could have called, too, with the alumnae arriving for homecoming.

MISS GOBLINETTE: Terrible, isn't it? Here are the letters you dictated earlier, Miss Magicia. (*Puts letters on desk*)

MISS MAGICIA: My goodness, but you've been quick about them!

MISS GOBLINETTE: It's the new electric Ouija Board I'm using.

MISS MAGICIA: Oh, is it working out, then?

MISS GOBLINETTE: Working out? Why, it's the greatest piece of office equipment since the spirit duplicator! Now, if you'll just sign these, I can hand them to the eleven o'clock apparition. That way they'll go airmail.

MISS MAGICIA: All right. (*Signs letters*) Has Mrs. Spectre arrived yet?

MISS GOBLINETTE: Yes, she's waiting to see you now. (*Takes letters*)

MISS MAGICIA (*Excitedly*): Oh, Miss Goblinette, do you know who she is? Why, she's one of the most exclusive ghosts in the country! She haunts only the best houses. And she's thinking of enrolling her two daughters in my school. Oh, what a blot on the school's escutcheon *that* would be!

MISS GOBLINETTE: I'll show her in.

MISS MAGICIA: Do, dear, do! (MISS GOBLINETTE *goes to door and opens it.*)

MISS GOBLINETTE (*Speaking at door*): You may come in now. (*Ushers in* MRS. SPECTRE, *a very "grande dame" type with a lorgnette.*) Miss Magicia, Mrs. Spectre. (MISS GOBLINETTE *exits.* MISS MAGICIA *stands.*)

MISS MAGICIA (*Gushing*): Do be seated, Mrs. Spectre, and make yourself uncomfortable. May I get you some refreshment? A cup of hemlock, perhaps?

MRS. SPECTRE (*Imperiously*): I am not here to socialize, Miss Magicia. (*Sits in chair beside desk*) Let us get down to business at once. As you know, I am thinking of enrolling my daughters in your school, but before I reach my decision, I have some questions to ask.

MISS MAGICIA: I'm sure your daughters could do no better educationally than to sign on at Miss Magicia's Seminary for Young Spooks.

MRS. SPECTRE: Hm-m. I'm not so sure. I've heard very good things about the Academy of Hades for Unearthly Young Ladies.

MISS MAGICIA (*Disparagingly*): Oh, they have *some* sort of reputation, I grant you . . . but your daughters would find the living accommodations there most uncomfortable. Here, at Miss Magicia's, we have the finest dormitories available. Daily maid service, for example—so every room always has a fresh supply of cobwebs. An attic reached by a hidden staircase *and* two built-in dungeons, so the girls always have a place to go and relax. And, of course, a skeleton in every closet.

MRS. SPECTRE: Well, the accommodations do sound nice. But what I'm really interested in is the curriculum you offer. I insist on the highest academic standards for my daughters. After all, I myself was Phi Beta Cadaver.

MISS MAGICIA (*Ingratiatingly*): And I'm sure you graduated Magna Cum Laudanum, too. I assure you, Mrs. Spectre, we offer only the most advanced studies. In the freshman and sophomore years, of course, all the students take the same program: Introduction to Haunting, Basic Invisibility, Problems of Demonology—you know, a general survey of the inhumanities. But in their junior year they get to choose a major: Home Wreckonomics, Ancient Mystery, that sort of thing. Incidentally, if your daughters are the athletic type, we have an excellent program in broom riding.

MRS. SPECTRE (*Indignantly*): Broom riding! You don't think that I, who have haunted some of the finest houses in the country—that I, who am a direct descendant of the Headless Horseman of Sleepy Hollow, and can trace my lineage all the way back to the Witch of Endor—would allow my daughters to do anything so common as riding brooms!

MISS MAGICIA (*Meekly*): They could ride sidesaddle.

MRS. SPECTRE (*Rising*): No, Miss Magicia, I'm afraid that you have a very mistaken idea of what would be acceptable to me in the way of education.

MISS MAGICIA (*Pleading*): Oh, wait, Mrs. Spectre. I'm sure if you met some of our star pupils you'd be convinced that the Seminary is *just* what you have in mind. (*Picks up phone, presses buzzer, and speaks into receiver.*) Miss Goblinette, ask a few of our star pupils to come to my office to meet Mrs. Spectre. (*Hangs up*)

MRS. SPECTRE: Well, they'll have to be spectacular if they're going to impress *me*.

MISS MAGICIA (*Confidently*): My dear Mrs. Spectre, my girls haven't made the National Halloween All-Stars for the past nine years in a row for nothing! (*Door opens*) Ah, here come the little darlings now. (WILMA WITCH, POLLY POLTERGEIST, *and* FANNY PHANTOM *enter and sit in the first, second, and fourth chairs at right.*) Thank you for coming, girls. I would like you all to meet Mrs. Horrible Nasty Spectre.

MRS. SPECTRE (*Quickly*): The third.

MISS MAGICIA: And these, Mrs. Spectre, are some of my star pupils. Wilma Witch. (WILMA *rises, curtsies, and sits.*) Polly Poltergeist. (POLLY *rises, curtsies, and sits.*) Gertrude Ghostess. (*She gestures to the third, empty chair. Nothing happens.*) And last, Fanny Phantom. (FANNY *rises, curtsies, sits.*)

MRS. SPECTRE (*Puzzled*): Excuse me, Miss Magicia—but you mentioned four girls. I see only three.

MISS MAGICIA: Oh, excuse me. I should have realized! Gertrude Ghostess has been doing her term paper on invisibility—and she's completely wrapped up in her work.

MRS. SPECTRE (*Skeptically*): I admit, Miss Magicia, that I would be very much impressed with your school if I thought you could really teach your ghostesses to be invisible. But I'm afraid I don't believe it. Admit it, Miss Magicia. There's nobody sitting in that chair.

MISS MAGICIA (*Gaily*): You're right! There's no *body* sitting in that chair. (MRS. SPECTRE *glares at her.*) Just my little joke. (*Calling*) Gertrude! Demonstrate to Mrs. Spectre that you are, indeed, in the room. (MRS. SPECTRE *begins shrieking and jerking her head, as though her hair were being pulled.*) There! You see? We don't call Gertrude the school spirit for nothing!

MRS. SPECTRE: Oh! Oh! Stop it! Stop it at once! (*Recovering*) My! (*In admiration*) She certainly is the ghostess with the mostest! Though I must say she could have done something less violent than pull my hair.

MISS MAGICIA (*Indulgently*): Well, ghouls will be ghouls, you know. Now, who wishes to be next to show Mrs. Spectre what she has learned here at the seminary?

WILMA (*Waving her hand*): I will, Miss Magicia.

MISS MAGICIA: Very well, Wilma. (*To* MRS. SPECTRE) Wilma is majoring in Languages. As a matter of fact, she won the National Witch Open Spelling Bee. Wilma, show Mrs. Spectre how well you can spell.

WILMA (*Rising*): Yes, Miss Magicia. (*Waves her hands as she speaks.*)
Tail of monkey, funeral knell,
None escape this witch's spell.
Wing of bat and eye of newt,
Let this lady now be mute.
(*She sits down primly.*)

MISS MAGICIA (*Enthusiastically*): Wasn't that a wonderful spell, Mrs. Spectre? My, it takes me right back to the dear, dead days of the Middle Ages!

MRS. SPECTRE (*Unable to speak*): Mmf! Mm-mf!

MISS MAGICIA: What's that, Mrs. Spectre?

MRS. SPECTRE (*Trying desperately to speak*): Mm-m-m-f-f-f! Mm-m-f-f!

MISS MAGICIA: Oh, of course! You can't speak because of Wilma's spell! She left *me* quite speechless, too! (MRS. SPECTRE *glares at her.*) Just my little joke. Wilma, dear, cast another spell, so that Mrs. Spectre can talk again.

WILMA: I don't feel like it.

MISS MAGICIA (*Overly sweet*): Wilma, dear, do as I ask— or I'll have to punish you by putting you on short rations. You know what that means, dear. No bones for a month —and no cream in your coffin, either.

WILMA (*Petulantly*): Oh, all right. (*Chants*)
Griffin's liver, lion's lung,
Let Mrs. Spectre use her tongue.

MISS MAGICIA: That's better.

MRS. SPECTRE (*Enthusiastically*): Oh, that was wonderful! Wonderful! I really must remember that—how did it go? "Tail of monkey, funeral knell . . ."

MISS MAGICIA: Now, Fanny Phantom, show Mrs. Spectre what you've learned in Shriekology. (FANNY *makes unearthly noises, gives a cackling laugh, and ends with a blood-curdling scream.*)

FANNY: Ooooooooooooooooooooo! Yeh-heh-heh-heh-ha-ha-ha! Or-r-r-r-r-r-r-r-g-g-g-g-g-h-h!

MRS. SPECTRE (*Shivering*): Marvelous! Marvelous! Why, she positively made my blood run warm!

MISS MAGICIA: Yes, she's very talented. Although I must admit I can't take all the credit for Fanny's skills. She took part in our Junior Year Abroad program—spent last semester studying at some of England's most notable haunted castles.

FANNY (*Proudly*): I even took a graduate seminar at the Tower of London.

MISS MAGICIA: And now it's Polly Poltergeist's turn. Polly, do your stuff!

POLLY (*Timidly*): I—I'm not sure I can really do much, Miss Magicia. I've been sick.

MISS MAGICIA: Oh, I'm sorry to hear it.

POLLY: I went on a field trip—and I'm afraid I caught a warm.

MISS MAGICIA: Well, try your best, dear. I'm sure Mrs. Spectre will understand.

POLLY: Very well. (*In a timid voice*) Sha-zam.

MRS. SPECTRE (*Loftily*): And what, may I ask, was that supposed to be?

POLLY: It—it didn't work.

MISS MAGICIA: Try again, dear. And really put some energy into it.

POLLY: Sha-zam. Sha-zam, sha-zam, sha-zam! (MISS MA-GICIA's *desk gives a tiny jump.* MISS MAGICIA *causes this with her foot.*)

MISS MAGICIA (*Enthusiastically*): Did you see that, Mrs. Spectre? My desk jumped.

MRS. SPECTRE: Humph! I *hardly* consider that much of a demonstration. I am *not* impressed.

MISS MAGICIA (*Hastily*): Polly, dear, as you're not feeling well, maybe you ought to try something a little less strenuous than table-turning. How about a nice little disembodied knocking sound?

POLLY (*Tentatively*): All right. I'll try. (*Recites*) Abra-cada-bra, knock, knock, knock. (*There is a loud knocking on door right.*)

MISS MAGICIA (*Happily*): Good girl, Polly! (*Loud knocking is repeated.*)

MRS. SPECTRE: Well, I must admit that was a good deal better. (MISS GOBLINETTE *enters right.*)

MISS GOBLINETTE: Excuse me for just walking in like this, Miss Magicia—but I knocked twice and nobody an-swered.

MRS. SPECTRE (*Rising indignantly*): Well! So it wasn't the girl's doing after all. (*Icily*) Miss Magicia, if this is the level of skill your seminary practices, I'm afraid there isn't a ghost of a chance of enrolling my girls with you.

MISS MAGICIA (*Upset*): Oh, Mrs. Spectre, I'm sure we can settle this problem to your complete satisfaction. Let me just see what my secretary wants, and then I'll give you my undivided attention.

MISS GOBLINETTE: It's the alumnae, Miss Magicia. (*To* MRS. SPECTRE) They've begun to arrive for our annual Halloween Homecoming. (*To* MISS MAGICIA) Apparently there's been some mixup over the housing arrangements.

MISS MAGICIA: Oh, dear! What seems to be the trouble?

MISS GOBLINETTE: Well, Queen Elizabeth the First and Bloody Mary both insist on staying in the Dormitory of the Seven Gables—but I can't get the girls from Salem to give up their rooms.

MRS. SPECTRE (*Impressed*): Did you say Queen Elizabeth and Bloody Mary?

MISS GOBLINETTE (*Continuing*): Then there are the graduates who belong to the Demons of the Ancient Regions . . .

MRS. SPECTRE (*Ecstatically*): Oh, the D.A.R.!

MISS GOBLINETTE: And as for the three weird sisters—

MRS. SPECTRE (*Interrupting*): Oh, Miss Magicia, I've changed my mind! Certainly my daughters must enroll here. Why, I had no idea that you have educated so many of the most fashionable spirits of all time!

MISS MAGICIA (*Surprised*): Why, Mrs. Spectre, I thought you knew. After all, you know our school motto. Girls?

WILMA, FANNY and POLLY (*In unison, hands over hearts*): High Goals—High Society—High Spirits!

MRS. SPECTRE (*Radiantly*): Just think! Why, if my girls come here—they might even end up in "Who's Who in Haunting!" (*Blackout*)

THE END

The Incredible Housing Shortage

Selling real estate for beans

Characters

SEYMOUR, *real estate broker*   BESSIE, *a cow*
PETER, *one of his tenants*   JACK, *a land salesman*

SETTING: *The Mother Goose Real Estate Office. There is a desk at left center, with a pile of papers and telephone on it. Up center is an open window. There is a door down right. Several office chairs are placed around room.*

AT RISE: SEYMOUR, *a harried real estate broker, is going through piles of papers, reading them aloud, and shaking his head as he does so.*

SEYMOUR (*Reading*): Wanted, studio apartment. Must be completely free of insects. Signed, Little Miss Muffet. (*Reads another slip*) Wanted, castle or palace, with kitchen privileges. Signed, the Queen of Hearts. (*Another slip*) Wanted, room to rent, preferably in the vicinity of the Y.W.C.A. Signed, Georgie Porgie. (*Phone rings. He picks it up.*) Mother Goose Real Estate Office. . . . Oh, hello, Mother Goose. What can I do for you today? . . . What? . . . You must be kidding! An old woman with twenty-seven children has moved into town and you want me to find them a place to live? Mother Goose, there isn't a vacant room, apartment, cottage or castle in all of Mother Goose Land. . . . Why, I'm in need of a bigger place to live myself. My house is so small, we have to keep our rock-a-bye baby in the treetop—and let me tell you, it's no joke trying to climb a tree when it's time for the kid's three o'clock feeding. . . . I'll tell you what I'll do. Let me call one of the giants over in Fairy Tale Land. Maybe one of them will give me an old shoe they can live in. . . . Yes, I'll try. . . . Oh, tell her not to worry about the rent. She'll be able to manage on a shoestring. . . . O.K., Mother Goose. And say, you wouldn't consider letting your geese sleep out of doors, would you? I know somebody who'd just love to live in that little chicken coop of yours. (*Looks at receiver, puzzled*) She hung up on me! (*Hangs up*) This is the worst housing crisis we've ever had. Everyone needs a place to live, and there's just nothing available! (*Knock at door is heard.* SEYMOUR *calls out.*) Come in, come in! (PETER *enters down right.*) Ah, Peter Peter! What can I do for you today?

PETER (*Glumly*): I'm here to pay the rent on that miserable thing you call a house.

SEYMOUR (*Taken aback*): Why, what's wrong with it?

PETER: Have *you* ever tried keeping house in a pumpkin shell? Seymour, you have to find us another place to live. My wife is threatening to leave me if we have to stay there.

SEYMOUR: What are you complaining about? Look at the butcher, the baker, and the candlestick maker. All I could find for them to live in was a two-room efficiency tub. Count your blessings!

PETER: My wife doesn't see it that way. She says the vacuum cleaner keeps filling up with pumpkin seeds. And she hates the color.

SEYMOUR: I think orange is a very nice color.

PETER: With purple wall-to-wall broadloom and pink slip-covers?

SEYMOUR (*Doubtfully*): I'll put you on the list, and if anything comes in, I'll let you know. But I wouldn't get my hopes up. I promised Little Boy Blue I'd get him out of that haystack of his before winter. And then there's Percy. . . .

PETER: Where do you have *him* living?

SEYMOUR (*Solemnly*): Ding, dong, bell, Percy's in the well. (*Briskly*) Now then, to business. I think you said you came to pay the rent. That's forty-five pieces of nine.

PETER: Pieces of nine? I thought it was pieces of eight.

SEYMOUR: Inflation, my boy, inflation.

PETER (*Glumly*): Not that it matters. I can't pay you in cash this month, anyway.

SEYMOUR (*Sighing*): Nobody can *ever* pay me in cash. Mother Hubbard pays in dog food, Little Jack Horner in plums. What's your offer going to be?

PETER: A cow. (*Calls out window*) Here, Bessie! (BESSIE *sticks her head through open window.*)

BESSIE: Moo-o-o!

SEYMOUR: A cow! What on earth am I going to do with a cow?

PETER: That's your problem. I really hate to give her up— I got her at a terrific price down at the secondhand cow lot. But my wife won't let me keep her. She says we're poor enough without having to feed a cow. She says she doesn't want some animal eating us out of house and pumpkin. (*To* BESSIE) O.K., Bessie, go munch some daisies. (BESSIE *withdraws her head.*)

SEYMOUR: Why did I ever go into this crazy business? People wanting houses to rent when there are no houses available. People paying me in animals instead of money.

I tell you, I'd sell this business for a handful of beans! (*There is a knock at the door.*) See who that is, will you? (PETER *opens door.* JACK *enters. He is a fast-talking, brash, salesman type.*)

JACK: Hello, folks. Jack's the name, construction's the game. Homes and houses, shacks and shanties, castles and cottages—we build 'em, you buy 'em. Who are you?

PETER: I'm Peter Peter.

JACK: Don't repeat yourself, Peter. I heard you the first time.

PETER: No, that's my name. Peter Peter.

JACK: That's the silliest thing I ever heard of. Who uses the same name twice?

PETER: Everyone around here does. Tom Tom the piper's son . . . Mary Mary quite contrary.

SEYMOUR: And I'm Seymour Seymour, the real estate salesman. What can I do for you?

JACK: You can talk business with me. I understand you have a bit of a housing shortage here.

SEYMOUR: That's the understatement of the year.

JACK: Well, my friend, your troubles are over. I'm here to sell you the most fantastic piece of acreage you ever laid eyes on. What would you say to five hundred open house lots, title free and clear, with city water, the most beautiful building land you ever saw—and all within easy commuting distance of downtown Mother Goose Land?

PETER: You must be kidding. There's no such property around here.

SEYMOUR (*Nodding*): You're right. Tell me, Jack. In which direction does this marvelous property of yours lie—that way? (*Points left*) Or that way? (*Points right*)

JACK: That way. (*Points up*)

SEYMOUR: How's that again?

JACK: Yes, my friends, the land I am talking about lies right over your heads. Acres and acres—just waiting to be developed—right above the clouds. I have the air rights all sewn up.

SEYMOUR: How could anybody build houses in the sky?

PETER: How could anybody even get up there to look around?

JACK (*Hurt*): Where's your faith, men? Why, I'm offering you the chance of a lifetime. Five hundred house lots—worth sixty thousand gold pieces on the open market. But you look like nice fellows, so I'm willing to let the whole thing go for three and a half bucks.

PETER: This guy should be working down at the second-hand cow lot.

SEYMOUR: If this land you have is as good as you say, how come you don't develop it yourself? Didn't you say you were a builder?

JACK: You've heard of the house that Jack built, haven't you? Well, I'm Jack.

PETER: So?

JACK: To be a builder, you have to have a keen mind, and strong determination, and an iron will to succeed. That used to be me, boys. But the fight's gone out of me. I'm through . . . washed up . . . finished. You may not believe this, but you are looking at a man with a broken heart.

PETER: You lost your wife?

SEYMOUR: You lost your girl?

JACK: I lost my cow. Bossy—best friend a boy ever had. (*Sighs deeply, puts his hand over his heart, shakes his head*)

SEYMOUR: Sounds like a tragic tale.

PETER: Tell us about it. It'll make you feel better.

JACK: It was like this. I was a poor boy, living alone with my widowed mother. We didn't have much money. Oh,

I used to make a few pennies now and then, helping fetch pails of water over at the water bottling plant. But one day I fell down and broke my crown, and that was the end of that. Mother tried taking in floors to wash—but then the recession came along. Finally, when there was nothing left to eat, I decided to sell old Bossy. I hated to do it—but you can see I had no choice.

SEYMOUR (*Sympathetically*): Sure, sure.

PETER: We know how it is.

JACK (*Dramatically*): Never will I forget the look on old Bossy's face when I sold her. I loved that cow, I tell you —and yet I betrayed her. I could tell from the way she mooed goodbye that I was breaking her heart. It was a moo so blue, I knew we were through. After that, my luck changed. Things began to go my way. I became a rich man, a successful businessman. And for a long time, I forgot about Bossy. But lately, I just can't get her out of my mind. Why shouldn't she be here with me to share in my good fortune? Here I am, sitting on top of the world—and for all I know, poor old Bossy's spending her last days in misery and hunger. I can never forgive myself for having sold her. (*Breaks down in sobs*)

BESSIE (*Sticking head in window*): Moo-o-o!

JACK (*Jumping up*): What was that?

PETER: That was only my cow, Bessie.

SEYMOUR: You mean that was only *my* cow, Bessie.

JACK (*Running to* BESSIE): Is it—? Could it be—?

BESSIE: Moo-o-o-o-o!

PETER: Quiet, Bessie.

JACK: This isn't Bessie! This is Bossy! (*Throws arms around* BESSIE) Oh, Bossy, Bossy, to think I've found you after all these years! (*To others*) Say, which of you two fellows owns this cow?

SEYMOUR: Why—I do.

JACK: Will you sell her to me? You *must* sell her to me! You've heard my tragic tale! Surely you wouldn't be so heartless as to keep me from being reunited after all these years with the only one I ever loved!

SEYMOUR (*Puzzled*): Well, technically, I'm afraid, she belongs to the real estate agency. After all, she *is* just a month's rent.

JACK (*Excitedly*): Then sell me the real estate agency! How much will you take for it?

SEYMOUR: It isn't worth anything.

PETER: Yes, it is, Seymour. You said you'd sell it for a handful of beans.

JACK: Sold! One handful of beans, coming right up. (*He pulls handful of beans from pocket and gives beans to SEYMOUR.*)

SEYMOUR: You don't waste time making up your mind, do you?

JACK: That's me—Jack be nimble, Jack be quick! (*Gleefully*) At last, my own real estate agency and my own cow!

PETER: But I thought you wanted to get out of business.

JACK: Now that I have Bossy again, the old fight is back. I'm going on to bigger and better things. Jack's the name, construction's the game!

SEYMOUR: Let me tell you something, Jack. You're a fool. You can't build houses in the sky—and without houses, you don't have a business. I tell you, this agency isn't even worth beans! (*He throws beans out window.*) But you wanted it, and now you have it. I can't tell you what a relief it is to me to be out of it. (*Phone rings.*)

JACK (*Happily*): My first customer!

SEYMOUR: What good are customers if you don't have any houses? Come on, Peter Peter. Let's get out of here.

PETER: I hate to admit it, Jack, but I think Seymour Seymour is right. Still, good luck to you.

SEYMOUR: He'll need it! (PETER *and* SEYMOUR *exit as* JACK *picks up phone.*)

JACK (*Into phone*) Mother Goose Real Estate. . . . Oh, I'm sorry, he just left. This is the new manager, Jack— I mean, Jack Jack. . . . What's that? You want a split-level ranch with four bedrooms, all-electric kitchen, indoor-outdoor recreation area, and a swimming pool? (*Behind the window, next to* BESSIE's *head, a beanstalk can be seen rising.*) . . . Yes, madam, I think we can help you. . . . Well, we don't have one right now, but I believe there's one going up very soon. . . . Oh, it's in a lovely section of town. This place is so beautiful, it'll have you walking on air. Did you ever hear of a place called Beanstalk Acres?

BESSIE (*Happily*): Moo-o-o! (*Quick curtain*)

THE END

Spying High

The case of the not-so-secret agents

Characters

PRIME MINISTER OF GLOCCA-MAURETANIA
FRITZ
HOUSEKEEPER
AGENT B-8-W

SETTING: *Living room of the Prime Minister's home. A desk with a blotter pad and a telephone on it stands at right, and a sofa is at left center. There is a rug on the floor.*
AT RISE: PRIME MINISTER, *who is heavily bearded, is talking on the phone.*

PRIME MINISTER (*Into phone*): Your Excellency, the situation is critical. The soldiers, the militia, and the sailors are in revolt. And the Queen is in the parlor, eating bread and honey. You know how she's always counted her calories. If she's eating bread and honey, it's a sure sign that she's given up hope. I tell you, we are on the eve of revolution, and our beloved country, Glocca-Mauretania, is about to go down the drain. . . . (*Strikes a pose*) Oh, you can count on me, Your Excellency. I know not what course others may take, but as for me, give me liberty or give me a passport so I can get out of this mess. . . .

Yes, Your Excellency, I intend to fly! To flee! (FRITZ *enters, dragging a huge steamer trunk.* PRIME MINISTER *notices him and continues talking into phone.*) As a matter of fact, my trusty old family retainer has just brought in my trunk. I must start packing this very instant. The boat leaves in twenty minutes, and if I'm not safely aboard, my life in Glocca-Mauretania won't be worth a plugged pfennig. Goodbye. (*Hangs up*)

FRITZ: Where do you want me to put this trunk, Your Prime Ministership?

PRIME MINISTER: Anywhere, anywhere. The important thing is to start packing at once. (*Emotionally*) Ah, Fritz, Fritz, my trusty old family retainer. Who'd ever have thought we'd be parting like this? But I must take it like a man. No time for sentiment. Let's get cracking with the packing.

FRITZ: Yes, Your Prime Ministership. What can I do?

PRIME MINISTER: Ring for the housekeeper. I have some instructions for her.

FRITZ: Yes, sir. (*He goes to back wall, pulls bell cord.*)

PRIME MINISTER (*To audience*): Notice how cleverly I got him to turn his back. Now, while he's not looking, I'll take these secret documents (*Pulls an envelope labeled "Secret Documents" out of his coat pocket*) and hide them. (*As* FRITZ *eavesdrops, exaggeratedly and obviously bending over and cupping his hand to his ear*) I know he's my trusty old family retainer—but in these troubled times, Glocca-Mauretania is overrun with spies. You can't be too careful. And if these secret documents should fall into enemy hands—ach! I shudder to think of the consequences. (*He hides envelope under desk blotter.*)

FRITZ (*Quickly resuming his dignified manner*): I have rung for the housekeeper.

PRIME MINISTER: Good, good. We've no time to lose.

(HOUSEKEEPER, *in floor-length black dress and white wig, enters.*)

HOUSEKEEPER (*In a high, creaky voice*): You rang, sir?

PRIME MINISTER: Ah, there you are, Mrs. Glockenspiel. Do you have my clothes ready?

HOUSEKEEPER: Everything is laid out in your bedroom, Your Prime Ministership.

PRIME MINISTER: Good, good. Come along, then, and help me carry the things down here. (*He and* HOUSEKEEPER *exit.*)

FRITZ: Aha! They've gone! (*To audience*) He thinks I'm a trusty old family retainer. Little does he realize that in actuality I am a—ha, ha!—spy. (*Goes to desk, takes envelope, hides it under rug, then holds his wrist watch to his mouth*) Hello, is this H.Q.? Agent 43½ here. I have the secret documents. Oops! Someone is coming. Must sign off now. (*He straightens up and majestically walks out down left, as* HOUSEKEEPER *enters up center, looks around, sees room is empty, comes downstage and speaks to audience.*)

HOUSEKEEPER (*In creaky voice*): They all think I'm the housekeeper, Mrs. Glockenspiel. Little do they realize that in actuality I am a—ha, ha!—spy. (*Straightens up and whips off wig, revealing male identity. Looks around, sees edge of envelope sticking out from rug, takes it, and hides it under sofa cushion. Pulls up skirt, revealing trousers, and takes walkie-talkie out of pocket*) Hello, is this Central Operations? Agent X.L.Y. here. I *have* the secret documents. More details later. Over and out. (*Looks around furtively, puts radio back into pocket, puts on wig, slinks out down right. Brief pause. Then, lid of steamer trunk rises.* AGENT B-8-W, *cloak-and-dagger type, emerges and looks around.*)

B-8-W (*To audience*): You guessed it, folks. I, too, am a—

ha, ha!—spy. (*Takes envelope from sofa, puts it under blotter on desk. Then takes off shoe and speaks into it*) Hello, is this Operations Scheduling? Agent B-8-W here. I *have* the secret documents. Wait! I think the Prime Minister is coming. I'll check back with you later. (*Goes out down left as* PRIME MINISTER *enters, followed by* FRITZ.)

PRIME MINISTER (*Going to blotter on desk and lifting it*): Ah, everything is just as I left it.

FRITZ (*Doing double take*): The documents! They're right where you left them!

PRIME MINISTER: How do you know where I left them, Fritz?

FRITZ (*Uncomfortably*): Would you believe E.S.P.?

PRIME MINISTER (*Blandly*): Not that it matters. You see, those aren't the real documents.

FRITZ: Those aren't the real documents?

PRIME MINISTER: No, that was just a dummy test. I had a feeling that this place was overflowing with spies. I wanted to be sure. Well, I guess I was wrong. Now I need have no fear of leaving the *real* secret documents.

FRITZ: You want me to turn my back again?

PRIME MINISTER: That won't be necessary. I've already hidden them—right in this very room. But why do I stand here chattering? I must fly! I must flee! I must get cracking with the packing! (*He goes out up center, carrying the envelope.*)

FRITZ: I must find those documents! (*He goes to desk and begins rummaging about in drawers.* HOUSEKEEPER *enters, goes to sofa, pulls up cushion.*)

HOUSEKEEPER (*In male voice*): Curses! The documents are gone!

FRITZ (*Looks up*): What do you mean, Mrs. Glockenspiel?

HOUSEKEEPER (*Startled, whirls around, puts on "creaky" voice*): Why—why, Fritz! I didn't notice you.

FRITZ (*Menacingly*): You're not Mrs. Glockenspiel, are you? (*Strides over and whips off* HOUSEKEEPER'S *wig*) You're—you're Charlie Culpepper!

HOUSEKEEPER (*Back in male voice*): How do you know my real name?

FRITZ (*Happily*): Don't you recognize me?

HOUSEKEEPER (*Looking at him closely*): It isn't—it isn't—

FRITZ: It is! Mervyn Mickle!

HOUSEKEEPER (*Shaking hands with him enthusiastically*): Merve, you old so-and-so!

FRITZ: Charlie, old buddy! Gee, it's good to see you! (*Suddenly*) But hush! Someone is coming! Quick, over here! (*They move to side of stage as* B-8-W *enters. He goes to desk, lifts blotter.*)

B-8-W: Curses! The documents! They're gone!

FRITZ *and* HOUSEKEEPER (*In unison*): Herbie Haliburton!

B-8-W (*In delighted surprise*): Hey! Imagine running into you guys here! (*They all gather together at center in a jovial, congenial group.*)

FRITZ: How many years has it been?

B-8-W: Not since the reunion five years ago, I think.

HOUSEKEEPER: It's just like old times. (*Nostalgically*) Oh, the happy, carefree years, when we were all students together at dear old S.M.U.

B-8-W (*Sighing*): Spy Master's University. Who ever dreamed we'd be running into each other like this? To think, we were undergraduates together—and here we all are on the same caper.

FRITZ: Say! How about singing the Alma Mater—for old times' sake?

HOUSEKEEPER: Good idea! (*They gather into a formal pose, facing front.*)

ALL (*Singing to the tune of "Far Above Cayuga's Waters"*):
Spying is a great profession,
Noble, good, and true.
So to join the great profession,
Come to S.M.U.
Learn the arts of cloak and dagger,
Mastering disguise.
And when you have graduated
Join the world of spies.

B-8-W: What memories it brings back! Sort of chokes me up.

FRITZ: Remember the time I almost flunked Introduction to Breaking Codes—and you tutored me, Charlie?

HOUSEKEEPER: Yeah, but it was you, Merv, that helped me with my Advanced Espionage. And good old Herbie, here—how would we ever have passed the Fingerprints Final if it weren't for him?

B-8-W: Say, I think we ought to write a letter to Dean Featheringill and tell him about how we all ran into each other like this. I'll bet he'd get a big kick out of it.

HOUSEKEEPER (*Soberly*): You mean you haven't heard?

B-8-W: Heard? Heard what?

HOUSEKEEPER: Poor old Dean Featheringill disappeared. Two years ago.

B-8-W (*Hat over heart*): Say, that's too bad. He was one of the great ones. Spying won't be the same without him.

FRITZ (*Happily*): Why don't we all go out and get ourselves some dinner tonight? We can really talk over old times then.

BOTH (*Ad lib*): Great! Good idea! Let's go! (*Etc.*)

HOUSEKEEPER (*Taking out walkie-talkie*): Let me call my office and tell them I'll be working late.

B-8-W (*Admiringly*): What a great unit! Gee, my outfit

must be way behind yours. I'm still using one of those old-fashioned shoe radios.

FRITZ: What about me? I'm stuck with a two-way wrist watch. That sort of thing went out with Dick Tracy!

HOUSEKEEPER (*Sitting down on edge of desk*): Let me get my call through, huh, fellows? (*As he sits, he knocks over a stack of books, revealing a Manila envelope.*)

FRITZ (*Rushing to it*): Look! Hidden among the books! The real secret documents! (*Holds up envelope on which is lettered* "Real Secret Documents.")

B-8-W (*Admiringly*): Gee, Mervyn, you graduated Number One in the class, and you're still the top spy. No wonder you got hold of the secret documents first.

FRITZ (*Handing the envelope to* HOUSEKEEPER): But they really belong to Charlie, here. After all, if he hadn't knocked over the books, we would never have seen them.

HOUSEKEEPER: Oh, but I couldn't take them, Mervyn.

FRITZ: But I insist, Charlie!

HOUSEKEEPER (*Taking envelope*): That's awfully nice of you. But I really think I ought to give them to Herbie. (*Hands envelope to* B-8-W.) After all, if it weren't for him, I'd never have graduated from Spy Masters University in the first place.

B-8-W (*Taking envelope*): Oh, really, Charlie, I couldn't accept this. (*Hands envelope to* FRITZ) No, Merv found them first. What's right is right. You both know Rule 27 in the Spy Manual as well as I do.

ALL (*Reciting in unison, hands over hearts*): Spy Manual Rule 27. Finders keepers, losers weepers.

PRIME MINISTER (*From offstage*): Fritz! Fritz! Where are you?

FRITZ (*Anxiously*): Someone's coming! Quick, you guys— hide! (HOUSEKEEPER *and* B-8-W *duck behind sofa as* PRIME MINISTER *enters.*)

PRIME MINISTER: Fritz, I've been looking all over for you. (*Suddenly*) But what's this? What's this?

FRITZ (*Blankly*): What's what?

PRIME MINISTER: You're holding the real secret documents! How on earth did you find them?

FRITZ (*Lamely*): I guess this is my day for E.S.P.

PRIME MINISTER: Well, you can just hand them over. I'm going to destroy them. I just had a telegram from the chief of staff. It seems the revolution has been canceled.

FRITZ: In that case, may I have the evening off? I want to have dinner with a couple of old friends I ran into.

PRIME MINISTER: Friends?

FRITZ: You can come out now, fellows. (HOUSEKEEPER *and* B-8-W *pop up from behind sofa.*)

PRIME MINISTER (*Looking at them a moment*): Well . . . all right, Fritz. You can have dinner with these men—on one condition.

FRITZ: What's that?

PRIME MINISTER: That you invite me to come along.

FRITZ: But what would a dignified old man like Your Prime Ministership have in common with these friends of mine?

PRIME MINISTER: You mean you haven't guessed? (*He whips off his false beard.*)

OTHERS (*Amazed; in unison*): Dean Featheringill!

PRIME MINISTER: Well, I'm sure not Mata Hari!

ALL (*Hands over hearts, singing*):
Spying is a great profession,
Noble, good, and true.
So to join the great profession,
Come to S.M.U.

(*Blackout and quick curtain*)

THE END

Equal Frights

Witches' liberation

Characters

FOUR SOLOS   SKELETON
MASTER MONSTER   VAMPIRE
GHOST   WEREWOLF
GHOUL   HORSEMAN
GOBLIN   MALE CHORUS
FOUR WITCHES

NOTE: *This oral reading play may also be easily produced as a stage play, if desired. The characters should wear Halloween costumes; no special set or properties are required.*

1ST SOLO:
  It happened in October,
  On October thirty-first.
2ND SOLO:
  The witches sent the word out—
  And the word it was the worst!
3RD SOLO:
  The warlocks and the werewolves
  Simply couldn't trust their ears.

4TH SOLO:
   The demons and the goblins
   Started crying in their biers.
1ST SOLO:
   The ghosts, they shook with fury;
   They screeched in angry tones.
2ND SOLO:
   The skeletons were rattled,
   And they shivered in their bones.
3RD SOLO:
   It couldn't be, it wouldn't be,
   It mustn't be, they cried!
4TH SOLO:
   But however hard they hollered,
   And however soft they sighed,
1ST SOLO:
   For a thousand-year tradition
   The death knell had been knelled.
2ND SOLO:
   They were beaten and they knew it.
   The witches had rebelled!
   (MALE CHORUS *murmurs angrily, ad lib.*)
MASTER MONSTER (*Clears his throat noisily*): My fellow
   monsters . . . ghosts, ghouls, and goblins . . . were-
   wolves, wizards and warlocks! As President of the Amal-
   gamated Federation of Haunters and Spooks, it is my un-
   happy task to inform you that owing to circumstances
   beyond our control, Halloween has been canceled.
GHOST: Canceled? Why?
GHOUL (*Louder*): Why?
GOBLIN (*Even louder*): Why?
MASTER MONSTER: Well, it seems that the witches have gone
   out on strike.

GHOST: A strike? That's ridiculous! How can they go out on strike? They're not even members of the Union.

MASTER MONSTER: I—er—I know. That seems to be one of their complaints. They think they should be allowed to join.

GHOUL (*Scornfully*): What? Let witches join the Union? That's the most ridiculous thing I ever heard!

GOBLIN: He's right! A witch's place is in the coven. Everyone knows that.

MASTER MONSTER: Well, they—they appear to reject that point of view. The witches seem to think that they should be treated as our equals. They—they call it witches' liberation.

GHOUL: Well, what are their demands? Maybe we can make a concession or two, and make them happy.

MASTER MONSTER: Oh, I don't think a concession or two is going to be enough. Their list of demands is really endless. They're calling for equal division of the cavework with their husbands . . .

MALE CHORUS (*In disbelief*): Shocking!

MASTER MONSTER: They want free night-care centers for the children . . .

MALE CHORUS: Ridiculous!

MASTER MONSTER: They want equal pay for equal haunting —and double time for after-midnight broom duty . . .

MALE CHORUS: Outrageous!

MASTER MONSTER: Oh, I assure you, they've written up quite a platform of equal frights.

GOBLIN: Are we going to let them get away with this?

MALE CHORUS: Never!

GHOST: Are we mice or are we monsters?

MALE CHORUS: Monsters!

GHOUL: I tell you, my fellow union members, if we let the

witches get away with this, there's no telling where it will end. Today, Halloween—tomorrow, the underworld!

MALE CHORUS (*Ad lib*): We must resist this outrage. Don't give in to 'em! How bold! (*Etc.*)

MASTER MONSTER: Gentlemen, gentlemen! Believe me, I sympathize with you. But the question is, how can we stop them?

1ST WITCH (*After a brief pause*): The question is, how can they stop us?

2ND WITCH: I don't know . . . but I still think canceling Halloween is risky.

3RD WITCH: I disagree, Hazel. Drastic ills call for drastic remedies. If we're ever going to get the monsters to see things our way, we must have a show of power.

2ND WITCH: But it's not as if things are so bad for us witches now. (*Flustered*) I mean, what's wrong with just being a plain old-fashioned witch?

1ST WITCH (*Outraged*): What's wrong with it? Everything! I didn't spend four years at college majoring in Shriek-ology just to spend the rest of my life over a steaming hot cauldron.

4TH WITCH: Right on, sister! We witches have talent and brains and ability! Yet when the average warlock looks at us, what does he see? Just another ugly face.

2ND WITCH (*Doubtfully*): But doesn't a warlock want to come home to a nice, quiet cave and a hot cooked brew after a hard day at the cemetery? Isn't that really a hag's noblest calling—to look after her warlock and raise his witchlets and make herself as ugly as she can?

3RD WITCH: Not on your broomstick, baby! We witches are the equals of any warlock alive—and it's time we de-manded our rights. We're tired of being treated as mere hex symbols.

4TH WITCH: That's why we're refusing to have anything to do with Halloween. That'll bring them to their senses!

2ND WITCH: But—but Halloween's tonight! The warlocks will never be able to do it all by themselves.

4TH WITCH: They're going to have to try.

2ND WITCH: But that's silly! Flying brooms, and carving jack-o'-lanterns, and rounding up the cats—well, that's witches' work.

1ST WITCH (*Sarcastically*): "Warlocks work from sun to sun, but witches' work is never done."

3RD WITCH (*Defiantly*): Let the monsters try to get Halloween going without our help. I'll bet that within an hour or two they'll come crawling on their knees!

2ND WITCH (*Puzzled*): Crawling on their knees? But that's how monsters always walk.

3RD WITCH: I was speaking figuratively, dear.

1ST WITCH: Well, Witch Hazel, are you with us?

2ND WITCH: Oh dear . . . I know you're right, but somehow it just doesn't seem—well—fair.

4TH WITCH: Fair? Why should we be fair to them?

2ND WITCH: I didn't mean that it was unfair to the monsters. I meant that it was unfair to the children. After all, Halloween *is* for children, you know.

4TH WITCH (*Contemptuously*): Huh! Don't talk to me about children! The last pair I ran into was a brother-sister act named Hansel and Gretel. What wretched little beasts! I fed them gingerbread and marzipan and frosting, and you know what thanks I got? They pushed me into the oven.

1ST WITCH (*Commiserating*): You must have been burned up about it.

4TH WITCH: I came pretty close to it.

3RD WITCH: Well, what do you say, girls? Do we let the warlocks try to get along without us—or do we go back to doing all the work and letting them get all the glory?

4TH WITCH: I say we strike!

1ST WITCH: Good! Let's all recite the Witches' Liberation Pledge.

WITCHES (*Together*):
Bubble, bubble, toil and trouble,
After midnight, pay us double.
Equal pay for equal fright—
Witches of the world, unite!
(*Short pause*)

SKELETON: How are things in Vampire Hollow? Is everything under control?

VAMPIRE: Oh, as good as can be expected. How are you guys making out down at the graveyard?

SKELETON (*With bravado*): Terrific! Of course . . . we *may* have to do without ghosts this year.

VAMPIRE (*Shocked*): No ghosts? On Halloween? How come?

SKELETON: Well—it seems their wives refused to do the laundry. They don't have any clean sheets.

VAMPIRE: Then why don't they just strip the linen off the beds and use that?

SKELETON (*Glumly*): They don't know how. Besides, do you have any idea how tough it is to be a ghost in a contour sheet? (*Slight pause*)

MASTER MONSTER: Well, how are the jack-o'-lanterns coming along?

GHOUL (*Discouraged*): Not so well, I'm afraid. I keep cutting myself with the scissors.

MASTER MONSTER (*Exploding*): Scissors! You don't cut out pumpkins with scissors, you nitwit!

GHOUL: You don't? Then how *do* you cut 'em?

MASTER MONSTER (*Meekly*): I—I'm not sure. Why don't you try nail clippers? (*Another pause*)

WEREWOLF: Do any of you guys know how to drive a broom?

GHOST: Well, I've never driven one, but it can't be too tough. I think you have to put it in "Neutral" first.

GOBLIN: Seems to me *my* wife always started it in "Sweep."

WEREWOLF: I've tried it both ways, and I still can't get it to turn over.

VAMPIRE: Idiot! You have to fill it with black cats first.

WEREWOLF (*Irritably*): Is that so? What kind of cats? Regular or hi-test?

VAMPIRE (*Meekly*): Here, kitty, kitty, kitty.

1ST SOLO:
The minutes turn to hours,
The night is drawing on.

2ND SOLO:
It soon would be the witching hour,
But the witches, they were gone!

3RD SOLO:
At first the warlocks faked it.
"Who needs those crones?" they cried.

4TH SOLO:
"We'll run All-Hallows by ourselves—
And take it in our stride!"

1ST SOLO:
But as the time went ticking on,
Faster and still faster,

2ND SOLO:
The truth became apparent:
It was leading to disaster!

SKELETON (*Outraged*): You want me to go up into that haunted house? By myself? Look, pal, I may be a skeleton, but I'm not out of my skull!

GOBLIN: If you think I'm going to go running around the countryside at all hours of the night, screaming at little kids, when I'd rather be curled up at the bottom of a nice dank swamp, you have another think coming!

GHOUL: Help! Help! The bats are loose and they're flying every which way! I can't catch them—and I'm afraid of bats! (MALE CHORUS *murmur discontentedly, ad lib.*)

MASTER MONSTER: My fellow monsters, we might as well surrender. We can never manage a decent Halloween without the witches. They've got us licked. I propose we send a delegate to them to tell them we humbly accept their terms. Is it agreed?

MALE CHORUS (*Ad lib, dispiritedly*): We know when we're beaten. Might as well give in. Let the witches have their way. (*Etc.*)

MASTER MONSTER: Where's the Horseman of Sleepy Hollow?

HORSEMAN: Here I am.

MASTER MONSTER (*Sadly*): On behalf of the entire membership of the Amalgamated Federation of Haunters and Spooks, I hereby authorize you to go to the witches, humbly, with your head in your hand, to accept whatever terms they demand. (*Short pause*)

WITCHES (*Ad lib, ecstatically*): We've won! They've surrendered! Right on, sister witches! (*Etc.*)

1ST WITCH: Well, girls, they've finally seen the light. It was a good fight—and we won it fair and square—which, I might add, is a very unusual thing for witches.

3RD WITCH: Let's not just stand around congratulating ourselves. There's work to be done. Halloween is only a few hours away. We have to get cracking if we're going to make it by midnight.

2ND WITCH: You see? I was right all along! You think you've won—but who's doing all the work, same as usual? Nothing's changed after all.

4TH WITCH: Oh, we may be doing all the work for Halloween—but this year, who do you think is going to stay behind in the cave for a change, doing dishes and changing diapers?

3RD WITCH: And that's only the beginning! We won't rest until every witch everywhere is the full equal of every warlock.

1ST WITCH: What do you mean, "every witch"? You don't think this is going to stop with witches, do you?

2ND WITCH: Why, whatever do you mean? Who are you going to liberate next?

1ST WITCH: How about fairy godmothers?

THE END

La Forza del Miss Muffet

A spoof of grand opera

Characters

MISS MUFFET   SCHMOENGRIN
EL SPIDER   GYPSIES
GYPSY QUEEN

NOTE: Music for all arias will be found in *Fireside Book of Folk Songs* and *Fireside Book of Favorite American Songs,* both edited by Margaret Bradford Boni and published by Simon and Schuster.

BEFORE RISE: *As an overture, pianist plays a stirring and highly emotional version of "Pop Goes the Weasel," "Three Blind Mice," or a medley of similar childhood songs.*

*   *   *

SETTING: *A woodland glade. The only necessary furniture is a tuffet—whatever that may be—at center stage.*

AT RISE: MISS MUFFET *enters, dressed in horned headdress and similar regalia of a Wagnerian soprano. She carries a bowl and spoon.*

MISS MUFFET (*In grand, declamatory manner used by all characters in play whenever they speak*): Ah! The sun is shining! The flowers are blooming! The breeze is breezing! What a beautiful afternoon for an opera! (*Sits on tuffet*) And what a wonderful way to begin an opera— by having lunch! (*Sings, to tune of "Cockles and Mussels"*)

I'm little Miss Muffet.
At mealtimes I rough it,
By eating my food in the heat of the day.
Though storms toss and buffet,
Brave little Miss Muffet
Sits tight on her tuffet and eats curds and whey.
I eat curds and whey, oh!
In the heat of the day, oh!
Whether sunny or cloudy, I eat curds and whey.

My strange reputation
Through all of the nation
Strikes fear in men's hearts, and it keeps them away.
So no one comes near me,
To frighten or cheer me,
Alone on my tuffet, I sit and I stay.
I'll huff it and puff it:
Brave little Miss Muffet
Sits alone on her tuffet
And eats curds and whey.

(*She eats.* EL SPIDER *enters, crosses downstage and sings.*)

EL SPIDER (*To tune of "I've Been Working on the Railroad"*):

I'm a happy bachelor spider.
Life for me is gay.
I'm a-singing and a-dancing,

All the livelong day.
Girls and such are not for me, sir,
Though some think they're great.
I'm as happy as can be, sir,
In my single state.

Happy as can be,
Happy as can be,
I enjoy a life that's wild and free.
Happy as can be,
Happy as can be,
Freedom is the life for me!
(*He turns, sees* MISS MUFFET, *who has been demurely eating her lunch, and he is instantly—and exaggeratedly —stricken by her loveliness.*) Oh, who art thou, radiant and ravishing creature?

MISS MUFFET (*Shrieking*): Ah-h! A spider! Go away! Go away!

EL SPIDER: Go away? But I adore—nay, I worship—nay, I *love* you! (*Sings, to tune of "Au Clair de la Lune"*)
In my whole life, never
A maid so fair I've seen.
Thou wilt live forever
In my heart a queen!
Say that you will have me!
Or my heart will break.
Let your heart be melted
For this spider's sake.

MISS MUFFET (*To "Au Clair de la Lune"*):
It may not be so, sir.
Love is not for me.
So, I pray thee, go, sir!
Leave my fancy free.
I know well that soft words

Only do deceive.
And I hate all spiders
For the webs they weave.

EL SPIDER (*To "Au Clair de la Lune"*):
Ah, my heart doth buffet
At one sight of you.
Let me share thy tuffet,
Gentle maiden, do!
Have you heard the proverb
That the wise men say:
"Where a bowl of curds is,
Love will find a whey."

MISS MUFFET (*Jumping up*): No, no! Begone, I say! This is
my personal, private tuffet, and I do not care to be dis-
turbed—by you, or by any man!

EL SPIDER: Nay, fair Miss Muffet. El Spider is not so easily
repulsed. For when once I love, I must go on loving, yea,
even if it be until death. (*She turns her back to him and
resumes seat, eating once more. He retires to side of stage
and strikes melancholy pose.* GYPSIES, *led by* GYPSY
QUEEN, *enter.*)

GYPSIES (*Singing to tune of "Waltzing Matilda"*):
Hail the gypsy chorus,
Singing songs in harmony,
Strolling along, for we've nothing to do.
But the leads in this opera
Need a chance to catch their breath.
Therefore we'll sing now
A chorus or two.

Oh, merry gypsies!
Ho, merry gypsies!
We've nothing to do with the plot of this play.
But without a gypsy chorus,

An op'ra's not an op-er-a.

So, merry gypsies, on stage we will stay.

GYPSY QUEEN (*Singing*):

In *Il Trovatore,*

We are used to set the scene.

In *Carmen* we're used in Act Two and Act Three.

In *The Gypsy Baron,*

We keep running in and out.

A chorus of gypsies is useful, you see!

GYPSIES (*Singing*):

Oh, merry gypsies!

Ho, merry gypsies!

We've nothing to do with the plot of this play.

But without a gypsy chorus,

An op'ra's not an opera.

So, merry gypsies, on stage we will stay!

(*They arrange themselves decoratively about stage.* EL
SPIDER *goes to* MISS MUFFET.)

EL SPIDER: Once more, fair maid, I beg you—give ear to my
pleadings! Reject me not again! After all, how many
chances do you get to marry a spider who's sung at the
Metropolitan Opera?

MISS MUFFET (*Scornfully*): You may think you're sharp, but
your proposal leaves me flat. (*Sings, to tune of chorus of
"Take Back Your Gold."*)

Leave me, I pray,

Thou strange and wicked spider.

Please go away.

My heart is made of stone.

Take back your words,

As sweet as apple cider.

Tuffets were made

So maids could dine alone!

EL SPIDER (*Resigned*): Ah! I see it was not meant to be!

*(Sings again to "I've Been Working on the Railroad,"
this time in a minor key)*

I'm a mournful bachelor spider.
Life for me is blue.
With a spider heart that's broken,
What am I to do?
I must go and find another,
Who will save the day.
One who'll honor, love, and cherish.
So I'm on my way.

(He starts to go out, but is stopped by an imperious gesture from GYPSY QUEEN.)

GYPSY QUEEN: Not so fast, El Spider! You can't just let a lady turn you down and then shrug and go on your way. Not in an opera, you can't. In an opera, when a lady turns you down, you die!

EL SPIDER *(Taken aback)*: Die! You've got to be kidding!

GYPSY QUEEN *(Ominously)*: A gypsy queen never kids!

GYPSIES *(To tune of chorus of "Waltzing Matilda")*:

Oh, merry gypsies!
Ho, merry gypsies!
When it comes to opera, we know the score.
And without a big death scene,
An op'ra's not an op-er-a.
So, merry gypsies, we'll tell you no more.

EL SPIDER *(Angrily)*: You mean I should die just because a bunch of gypsies sing a silly song?

MISS MUFFET *(Dramatically)*: No! You should die because it is so written in the ancient evil curse!

EL SPIDER: I never heard anything about an evil curse.

MISS MUFFET: I know you haven't. But here comes the great knight, Schmoengrin, to tell you all about it! *(*SCHMOENGRIN *enters, dressed in Wagnerian regalia. If desired, he may be pulled onstage in a toy wagon deco-*

rated with swan's head.) Tell him, Schmoengrin! Tell
him about the ancient evil curse!

SCHMOENGRIN (*To tune of "When Johnny Comes Marching
Home"*):
There is an ancient evil curse,
Hurrah! Hurrah!
From bad your life must go to worse.
Hurrah! Hurrah!
It is written down in words of fire.
Whoever raises Miss Muffet's ire
Must be doomed to death,
So sayeth the ancient curse.

The ancient curse goes on to say,
Hurrah! Hurrah!
The spider who with his life must pay,
Hurrah! Hurrah!
Will be known to all eternity
As a creature of ig-*no*-mi-*ny,*
So prepare for death!
So sayeth the ancient curse!

EL SPIDER (*Grumbling*): Well . . . if I *have* to, I have to!
But I still think it's rough.

SCHMOENGRIN (*Grandly*): Ah! But there is one reward!

EL SPIDER (*Hopefully*): There is?

SCHMOENGRIN: Yes! You get to sing a *Liebestod*—a great
duet of love and farewell!

EL SPIDER (*Valiantly*): So be it! If I must die, let me die
with a song on my lips!

MISS MUFFET (*To the tune of "Bill Bailey, Won't You
Please Come Home"*):
Now you must leave me, Spider.
Now we must part.
Here is my farewell song.

Say you forgive me, Spider.
Say you forgive!
I know I done you wrong!

EL SPIDER (*Singing*):
Of course I forgive, Miss Muffet!
How could I blame?
A love like ours was not to be!
But when I'm gone,
My tale will live on
In rhymes told in the nursery!
(*He seizes bowl from* MISS MUFFET, *drinks it down, and gasps.*) Ah! Poisoned! (*He dies.*)

MISS MUFFET (*Rapturously*): Schmoengrin!

SCHMOENGRIN: Miss Muffet! (*They embrace dramatically at center.*)

GYPSIES (*Shaking tambourines*): Hurrah! (*Quick curtain*)

THE END

Production Notes

My Son, the Prince

Characters: 4 male; 1 female.
Playing Time: 10 minutes.
Costumes: King Harold and Prince Engelbert wear royal attire. Both wear small crowns. The King has a long robe, and may carry a sceptre. Nanny wears a medieval gown, and a cap with a wimple. Fairy Godfather wears a long robe and carries a wand. Page is dressed appropriately.
Properties: None needed.
Setting: The throne room of King Harold's palace. Up center is a large throne; there is a small table down right, and some chairs scattered about. Rugs, draperies, etc., may be added as desired.
Lighting: No special effects.

Avon Calling!

Characters: 4 male.
Playing Time: 10 minutes.
Costumes: Jerry wears modern business suit. Marvin wears shirt and slacks. Shakespeare is dressed in black tights, black turtle-neck pullover and carries a skull. Bacon is dressed in tights, doublet with white ruff.
Properties: Skull, coffee mug.
Setting: A modern office. There is a cluttered desk at center, with telephone, typewriter, pens, pa-

pers, and letters on it. A large desk chair stands in front of it, and there are several occasional chairs around the room. There is a doorway down right.
Lighting: No special effects.

Meet Miss Stone-Age!

Characters: 1 male; 4 female.
Playing Time: 10 minutes.
Costumes: All characters wear imitation animal skin costumes. Rocky wears a top hat and a black bow tie tied around his bare neck. Glenda wears cave woman costume, spike-heeled shoes, dark glasses, and a tiara.
Properties: Hand microphone for Rocky (optional), bouquet of roses for Glenda, three caveman clubs (papier-mâché), huge stone wheel (papier-mâché), large slab of stone, chisel, slip of paper.
Setting: The stage of a beauty pageant, furnished and decorated as desired.
Lighting: No special effects.

Great Caesar's Ghost!

Characters: 4 male.
Playing Time: 10 minutes.
Costumes: Classical Roman togas. Caesar wears laurel wreath on his head.
Properties: Stenographer's pad and

167

pencil; crystal ball with "snow" in it.

Setting: Caesar's office. There is a desk with an office chair beside it at center, and a large executive-type chair behind it. Several other chairs stand around room.

Lighting: No special effects.

CINDERELLA REVISITED

Characters: 5 female.

Playing Time: 15 minutes.

Costumes: Medieval dress. Cinderella wears heavily patched dress and apron, with a dustcloth, potato, and paring knife in pocket. Fairy Godmother wears traditional costume, wings, overshoes and a tiara.

Properties: Carpet sweeper, potato, paring knife.

Setting: The living room of the Stepp home, a typical middle-class medieval dwelling. An archway up center leads to front door, left, and to rest of house, right. A fireplace is down left with oversized opening that is also an entrance. A mirror hangs above it. A telephone is on a table. Benches, stools, tables and spinning wheel complete the setting.

Lighting: No special effects.

A COUPLE OF RIGHT SMART FELLERS

Characters: 4 male.

Playing Time: 12 minutes.

Costumes: Zeke and Zack wear overalls and checked shirts. Harris and Carter wear stylish business suits, with handkerchiefs and wallets containing stage money in their pockets.

Properties: Two real-looking toy cats, wooden sign reading TURN-PIKE—5 MILES, stage money, map.

Setting: Yard in front of a Connecticut farmhouse. At left center there are two rocking chairs and a small straight chair with a cat sleeping on it. Exit at left leads to farmhouse; exit at right leads to road.

Lighting: No special effects.

THE THREE SWINE OF MOST SMALL STATURE

Characters: 4 male; 1 male or female for Stage Manager.

Playing Time: 10 minutes.

Costumes: Simple, stylized animal costumes for Pigs and Wolf. Stage Manager may wear Oriental jacket, cap, and long queue, or Oriental dress. For a simple classroom production no costumes are necessary.

Properties: Cut-out snowflake.

Setting: Bare stage, with a cut-out tree standing at one side.

Lighting: No special effects.

Sound: Gong, as indicated in text.

TRY DATA-DATE!

Characters: 5 male.

Playing Time: 10 minutes.

Costumes: Modern dress. The Date wears gorilla suit.

Properties: Paper and pencil; large telephone directory covered with plain paper; card.

Setting: Office of Data-Date. A desk and three chairs are at one side. Up center (or placed against opening in curtains, if skit is played before curtain) is the computer, a cardboard box large enough to conceal The Date, who hides in the box (or may enter from behind curtains through computer, if skit is played before curtain). Exterior of computer is covered with knobs, dials, switches, reels of tape, gears, lights, etc. A door is cut into the front. Exit is at one side.

Lighting: No special effects.
Sound: Dog barking and computer noise, as indicated in script.

THE ONCE AND FUTURE FROG

Characters: 2 male; 2 female.
Playing Time: 10 minutes.
Costumes: Traditional fairy tale costumes. Fred is dressed in green.
Properties: Flyswatter, pen, envelopes.
Setting: A room in King Marmaduke's castle. There is a large, low, open window in one wall. Next to it is a low chest. Near the chest there is a stool. Up center is a door leading to rest of castle. At left stand a writing desk and chair. Envelopes and pen are on table. Other chairs stand left and right.
Lighting: No special effects.

THE TEN-YEAR-OLD DETECTIVE

Characters: 4 male.
Playing Time: 10 minutes.
Costumes: Pete and John wear everyday clothes; Pete has a moustache. Mortimer and Marmaduke wear typical gangster outfits: double-breasted suits, dark shirts, light ties, and hats. Over suits they wear lobster bibs.
Properties: Magnifying glass; one green glove; telephone; can of powder.
Setting: The Peter Piper Detective Agency office, in Pete's house. A desk and chair, and another chair, are placed at center. A door is at one side.
Lighting: No special effects.
Sound: Telephone ringing, as indicated in text.

THE BRIDE OF GORSE-BRACKEN HALL

Characters: 3 male; 2 female.
Playing Time: 15 minutes.

Costumes: Any period, so long as it looks "dated," is acceptable. Dark housekeeper's dress for Mrs. Gargle. Wedding dress for Petunia. Workman's clothes for Atkinson. Dark suit and turned collar for the Vicar. White ruffled shirt and bow tie for Chichester; pulled over his legs is a fish tail, constructed on the style of a laundry-bag; the drawstring ties around his waist. The tail is painted green, and "scales" are painted on; a few large sequins can be sewn on, too.
Properties: Candle in candlestick for Mrs. Gargle, basket covered with burlap sack and bill for Atkinson, wheelchair, basket, and empty bottle for Chichester, prayer book for the Vicar.
Lighting: The stage is dim at first; when the drapes are opened, the lights become quite bright.
Sound: Foghorn, as indicated in text.

THE LAST TIME I SAW PARIS

Characters: 1 male; 3 female.
Playing Time: 10 minutes.
Costumes: Ancient Greek robes and sandals for goddesses. Athene wears a helmet. Paris wears a short tunic and sandals laced up to the knee.
Properties: Thunderbolts (cardboard cutouts), letters, postcard, golden apple.
Setting: Mount Olympus. There are stone benches right and left. There is an exit at one side.
Lighting: No special effects.

HEN PARTY

Characters: 5 female.
Playing Time: 15 minutes.

Costumes: Everyday dress, and appropriate animal half-masks.
Properties: None.
Setting: Living room of Henny Penny's house. At left center is a sofa. Tea table in front of sofa is set for tea, with cups, saucers, spoons, napkins and teapot. Up center, an arched doorway leads to the hall and front door. At right is a door leading to the rest of the house. Several comfortable chairs are arranged about the room.
Lighting: No special effects.

SAIL ON! SAIL ON!

Characters: 5 male; 1 female.
Playing Time: 15 minutes.
Costumes: Columbus is in period costume, with a plumed hat, sword, and other details in keeping with his melodramatic personality. Other characters may be in modern, everyday dress, or in period costumes, also.
Properties: Paper bag containing jewelry, including necklace, earring, silver I. D. bracelet; pen; steno pads and pencils for reporters; sketch pad for Frank.
Setting: Columbus's apartment in Spain. Plain wooden table, several broken-down chairs (Spanish style, if possible), and small cabinet furnish room. Exits are down left and down right.
Lighting: No special effects.

HAPPY HAUNTING!

Characters: 6 female.
Playing Time: 10 minutes.
Costumes: Halloween costumes, as appropriate, for all.
Properties: Letters for Miss Goblinette; lorgnette for Mrs. Spectre.

Setting: Miss Magicia's office. A desk, with a chair behind it and one beside it, are left center. Four straight chairs are arranged in a semicircle right, facing the desk. There is a door at right.
Lighting: No special effects.
Sound: Loud knocking, as indicated in text.

THE INCREDIBLE HOUSING SHORTAGE

Characters: 3 male; 1 female.
Playing Time: 10 minutes.
Costumes: Everyday, modern dress. If desired, characters may wear "fairy tale" costumes. Bessie wears cow-head mask.
Properties: Beans.
Setting: The Mother Goose Real Estate Office. An open window is up center and door is down right. A desk with pile of papers and telephone are left center. Several office chairs are placed about room. A thick green beanstalk is seen rising outside window at end of play.
Lighting: No special effects.
Sound: Telephone, as indicated in text.

SPYING HIGH

Characters: 4 male.
Playing Time: 15 minutes.
Costumes: Prime Minister wears a black suit; Fritz is dressed in work clothes; Housekeeper wears long, black dress and apron over man's clothes; and B-8-W wears everyday clothes. Prime Minister wears heavy, black beard, and Housekeeper, woman's wig.
Properties: Trunk, envelope labeled "Secret Documents," Manila envelope labeled "Real Secret Documents," transistor phone or walkie-talkie.

Setting: Living room of the Prime Minister's home. A desk with a telephone and a stack of books on it stands at right and a sofa at left center. There are various chairs around the room, and a rug on the floor. There are doors down right and down left and one up center. There is a bell pull on back wall.

Lighting: No special effects.

EQUAL FRIGHTS

Characters: 8 male; 4 female; 4 male or female for Solos; male extras for Chorus.

Playing Time: 10 minutes.

Costumes: Halloween costumes.

Properties: None required.

Setting: Bare stage. Appropriate Halloween decorations may be used if desired.

Lighting: No special effects.

LA FORZA DEL MISS MUFFET

Characters: 2 male; 2 female; as many male and female for Gypsies as desired.

Playing Time: 15 minutes.

Costumes: Miss Muffet and Schmoengrin wear Wagnerian outfits with horned helmets, shields, etc. Spider should have eight legs, and a lavish operatic costume. Gypsy Queen and Gypsies wear appropriate costumes and carry tambourines.

Properties: Bowl and spoon, and, if desired, a toy wagon decorated with a swan's head.

Setting: A woodland glade. There is a tuffet at center.

Lighting: No special effects.